滑1/a98

D1603041

4/98

CITADEL ON THE CHANNEL

"The Royal Presidio of Santa Barbara, 1791," continuing then an acrylic painting by Russell Antonio Ruiz. Courtesy Russell Clay Ruiz. Photo by Wm. B. Dewey.

CITADEL
ON THE
CHANNEL

The Royal Presidio of Santa Barbara,
its founding and construction,
1782-1798

by
RICHARD S. WHITEHEAD

edited, with an epilogue, by
DONALD C. CUTTER

THE SANTA BARBARA TRUST FOR HISTORIC PRESERVATION
and
THE ARTHUR H. CLARK COMPANY
1996

LIBRARY OF CONGRESS CATALOG CARD NUMBER 96-2105
ISBN 1-879208-02-4

Co-published by
Santa Barbara Trust for Historic Preservation
P.O. Box 388, Santa Barbara, CA   93102
and
The Arthur H. Clark Company
P.O. Box 14707, Spokane, WA   99214

Library of Congress Cataloging-in-Publication Data

Whitehead, Richard S.
    Citadel on the channel: the Royal Presidio of Santa Barbara, its founding and construction, 1768-1798 / by Richard S. Whitehead; edited, with an epilogue, by Donald C. Cutter.
        p.   cm.
    Includes bibliographical references and index.
    ISBN 1-879208-02-4
    1. Santa Barbara Presidio (Santa Barbara, Calif.)—History.
2. Fortification—California—Santa Barbara—History—18th century. 3. Historic buildings—California—Santa Barbara. 4. Santa Barbara (Calif.)—Buildings, structures, etc.
I. Cutter, Donald C.   II. Santa Barbara Trust for Historic Preservation.   III. Title.
F869.S45W34 1996   96-2105
979.4'91—dc20   CIP

Table of Contents

Illustrations

Acknowledgements

Many people contributed to the publication of *Citadel on the Channel*. Thanks must first go to Donald Cutter for undertaking the task of preparing the raw manuscript for publication with such sensitivity to its original author, Richard S. Whitehead. We would also like to acknowledge the contributions of the many persons whose critical reading of the original manuscript helped inform its final composition. They include Richard Ahlborn, John Drayton and his Univerity of Oklahoma Press reviewers, Diane Everett-Barbola, Bernard Fontana, Sasha Honig, Michael Imwalle, Jarrell Jackman, Mardith Schuetz Miller, James Mills, Norman Neuerburg, Richard Oglesby, Diane Spencer Pritchard, Robert Reese, and Charles Polzer, S.J.

A special debt of gratitude is owed to Norman Caldwell for his careful reading and editing of the manuscript's engineering details. Norman also provided the sketches of the chapel roof support system.

Michael Imwalle updated archaeological information in the text. Kathryn Masson sketched the Alta California Presidio brands. Ruth Caldwell and Jean Liston meticulously checked the manuscript for spelling and grammar errors. Catherine Rudolph served as editorial and publication coordinator.

Foreword

Citadel on the Channel is the product of one of the most committed Presidio enthusiasts, Richard S. Whitehead, a man whose engineering training and love of detail proved a great boon to the Presidio restoration at a critical juncture in its history during the 1970s. What emerges from a reading of this volume is an appreciation of the depth and breadth of inquiry required to undertake a historical reconstruction. Such a reconstruction has been the primary goal of the Santa Barbara Trust for Historic Preservation since its formation in 1963. Immersion in Spanish documents of the period, as well as a knowledge of archaeology and adobe technology, were the perfect challenges for the fertile mind of Richard Whitehead following his retirement in 1969 after twenty-two years as Santa Barbara County Planning Director.

From its early years to 1980, the Trust and the Presidio project were sustained primarily by volunteers such as Mr. Whitehead. These volunteer efforts included endless hours of time donated to working with city, county and state officials to set up funding sources and acquire land in the Presidio area. Also, a group called the "Presidio Volunteers" was instrumental in increasing community awareness of the Trust's restoration goals in the 1970s.

In 1980, the Trust, at the urging of Mr. Whitehead and others, decided to hire a professional staff to help advance the project. That staff has grown to include today a historian, curator, archivist and archaeologists. The 1980s also saw the first public outcries against the Presidio restoration—mostly from tenants and merchants who feared displacement as the project began to become a reality. It is a little ironic and tells us something about the times we live in that it took the original colonists about eight years to build the Presidio, while the Trust has been at its task of reconstruction for over twenty-five years. Perhaps it is some consolation to know that prior to the actual founding of Santa Barbara's Presidio in 1782, several years of letter exchanges took place between officials in Alta California and Mexico City on the subject of establishing Santa Barbara's Presidio. Also, in the process of re-creating Santa Barbara's Spanish military fortress, we have become acutely aware how deeply buried historical information is and how much has been forgotten from California's Spanish past.

Originally Mr. Whitehead intended to write a much longer volume than appears here, with chapters on archaeology, armaments, soldiers, daily life and the history of the Trust's involvement in the reconstruction. Alas, his final years were plagued by bouts of ill health and the manuscript was left uncompleted when he died in 1988. Fortunately, Mr. Whitehead had the foresight to see that his work would have to be carried on by others, and he made the generous offer of donating his research collection, amassed over a twenty-year period, if the Trust would set up a research archive.

This facility is now open and operating in the Presidio State Park. It is overseen by a Research Center Committee, which, out of respect for Mr. Whitehead's enormous contribution, set as a top priority the publication of *Citadel on the Channel*. As a first step, the Committee decided to circulate it among scholars for comment. The responses were extremely favorable with one of the readers, Professor Donald Cutter, offering to prepare the manuscript for publication. Dr. Cutter felt strongly that the work should be left as much as possible in Mr. Whitehead's own words. Dr. Cutter and others also recommended dropping the two opening chapters on Old Spain and New Spain. These are the only significant changes to the manuscript. As part of his work, Dr. Cutter checked for accuracy all book citations and references, made minor editorial changes and wrote the epilogue.

For the most part, the research for *Citadel on the Channel,* which was written over a period of half a dozen years, has stood up to subsequent research and archaeology, although there are a few statements which have been contradicted by more recent information that has come to light. For example, we know now that many Spanish period churches had sloped floors, while Mr. Whitehead assumed the Presidio Chapel floor should have been level. Mr. Whitehead would have been the last person to worry about this, because he knew many of his findings were tentative and subject to revision. What he was most concerned with was setting standards for serious research, and on this score he gets high marks.

Citadel on the Channel is a testimony to what can be achieved by volunteers convinced of the importance of historical memory. The Presidio's living history program exemplified by "Una Pastorela" (our Christmas play) and Presidio Days; our archaeological research lab, including the computer cataloguing program that has been set up in it; the ongoing archaeological excavations; the rebuilding underway of the Presidio buildings north of Canon Perdido Street; and the Trust research and translation programs being generated in cooperation with UC Santa Barbara are all projects built on the foundation laid by the work of Richard Whitehead. Were he with us today I know he would be pleased with the progress we are making. We at the Trust in turn are indeed grateful to him for his enormous contribution to El Presidio de Santa Barbara and to the Santa Barbara Trust for Historic Preservation.

JARRELL C. JACKMAN, Ph.D.
Executive Director
Santa Barbara Trust for Historic Preservation

Preface

During my twenty-two years' service as Santa Barbara County Planning Director, I became interested in the county's early history, particularly in the names and locations of Indian villages that existed when the Spanish explorers arrived. Subsequently, my interest shifted to the events leading up to settlement of the county by the Spanish. My career with the county allowed little time for research in these fields. So when I retired in April 1969, I was ripe for any intriguing project that would open new vistas in local history.

One summer day a few weeks after I retired, I was strolling down East Canon Perdido Street in Santa Barbara when I was hailed by a friend working as a volunteer on the archaeological excavations of the Santa Barbara Royal Presidio Chapel. The presidio, or fort, was founded in 1782, and the chapel, built a few years later, was its principal building. Knowing of my recent liberation from the daily grind and being familiar with my engineering background, he asked if I would survey in a grid system for the project. This grid is a checkerboard series of lines laid out on the ground to permit archaeologists to record the horizontal and vertical locations of foundations and artifacts uncovered in their work. It is an essential feature of any "dig." The idea appealed to me, and I agreed to become a volunteer and subsequently joined the loosely-knit organization called "The Volunteers of the Santa Barbara Royal Presidio." This casual encounter changed my entire retirement life and gave me an absorbing interest in the events that dominated the first third of the city's existence.

After completing the survey for the chapel site and participating in archaeological excavation, I extended the survey into the four blocks in which the presidio was located, the area bounded by Carrillo, Garden, De la Guerra and Anacapa Streets, and assisted in the discovery of the original presidio foundations on all four sides of the presidio quadrangle. Subsequently I was appointed a member of the Board of Trustees of the Santa Barbara Trust for Historic Preservation, the nonprofit organization spearheading reconstruction of the presidio compound.

Being of an inquisitive mind, I began delving into history books to learn more of the presidio's role in the city's early development. I soon discovered there was a dearth of reliable information about the presidio and that there were differing opinions as to the veracity of much of the available information. Furthermore, authorities held conflicting views concerning many historical details and events related to the presidio. Gradually, my interest in discovering what was fact and what was myth became almost obsessive, and I wound up with what every retiree should have to insure a long and satisfying life in retirement: a worthwhile and absorbing interest that would challenge whatever abilities I had as a researcher, historian and writer.

The objectives of the Trust for Historic Preservation as expressed in its articles of incorporation are to acquire, protect, preserve and, where appropriate, reconstruct historical sites and structures throughout Santa Barbara County. However, the primary interest of the Trust for Historic Preservation is the Santa Barbara Presidio and its reconstruction in as authentic a manner as archaeology, historical research, funds and the building code permit. This mandates extensive knowledge of the methods and materials of construction used in the original structures, subjects concerning which very little has been written, especially with regard to the Santa Barbara Presidio buildings.

Discovery of two manuscript reports written in the 1930s describing the history and reconstruction project at Mission La Purísima Concepción near Lompoc diverted me into preparation of these reports for publication. Besides recounting the mission's history, the reports detailed the materials and methods of construction used in the original 1813 structures as revealed by archaeological excavations, plus materials and methods of construction used by the Civilian Conservation Corps personnel when the mission was reconstructed in the 1930s. Following its founding in 1787, La Purísima Mission structures were destroyed by earthquake in 1812. The mission was reconstructed at its present location in 1813. The information contained in these reports was invaluable in insuring authenticity in reconstruction of the Santa Barbara Presidio, built roughly contemporaneously. My diversion came to an end in 1980 with publication by the Santa Barbara Trust for Historic Preservation of the book entitled *An Archaeological and Restoration Study of Mission La Purísima Concepción*, which I edited and prepared for publication. It contained the two reports written for the National Park Service by Fred C. Hageman, Architectural Foreman, and Historian Russell C. Ewing.[1]

I had already decided that a comparable book on the Santa Barbara Presidio was needed and that this would be a good "retirement project" for me to undertake. Because of conflicting opinions concerning details of the presidio's early period, I resolved from the beginning to make every effort to prove or disprove all statements, conjectures and conclusions I read or was told, regardless of their source, by referring to original

---

[1]Hageman and Ewing, *An Archaeological and Restoration Study of Mission La Purísima Concepción*, Whitehead (ed.). All works in the notes are cited in full in "Sources" at the end of this study.

documents. Where original documents failed to provide the facts, findings from archaeological excavations would sometimes provide the answer. If proof were still lacking, conclusions would be drawn from examples at other mission-period buildings, or by reference to the most reputable secondary sources or from what, in my opinion, was logical and made common sense.

This had been the process followed in the reconstruction of La Purísima Mission in the 1930s. Reminiscences, unless written down at the time the event occurred, were discounted because of the risk of faulty memories. Such recollections should be recorded but not indicated as incontrovertible. Too often, a writer will present conjecture as absolute fact in order to make his story colorful and fascinating. His statements will be repeated by others and go down through the years unchallenged simply because others failed to spend the necessary time to research the facts.

The incentive to write this book came from a desire to present reliable historical information from original documentary sources. The reconstruction of the entire presidio could then be accomplished with greater authenticity even though only the foundations and two buildings have survived. Also, I wanted to record the material I had discovered in order that duplication of time and effort by other presidio researchers be avoided as much as possible. This book is replete with footnotes so that, as time goes on and additional source material is uncovered by others, an assessment of the validity of conclusions can be made based on the new information.

Of necessity, much of what I used as source material required translation. After considerable study, I still lacked confidence in my own translations. However, beginning in the 1960s, Mrs. Geraldine V. Sahyun had translated numerous presidio documents obtained from The Bancroft Library in Berkeley for the Santa Barbara Historical Society and the

Santa Barbara Mission Archive-Library. The most important was the 1788 map of the presidio signed by its commandant, Felipe de Goycoechea. Mrs. Sahyun has generously
allowed me to obtain and use copies of her translations. Over
a period of fourteen years, I have collected hundreds of pho-
tostatic, xerox and microfilmed copies of other presidio-
related documents from The Bancroft Library, the Santa
Barbara Mission Archive-Library and other sources. For
three years, I enjoyed the cooperation of a crew of volunteers
who translated documents I gave them. Other volunteers
typed the translations.

Without Mrs. Sahyun's output and the work of these
other volunteers, this effort would have been impossible, and
I wish to acknowledge my debt to all of them for their metic-
ulous, time-consuming and often frustrating labors. Most of
the volunteers were initially contacted through the cooperation of Mrs. Helen Paul, Director of the Retired Senior Volunteer Program (R.S.V.P.) in Santa Barbara. They included
Mrs. Robert Smitheram, Mrs. Ruth Adams, Miss Elaina
Graves, Mrs. Edna White, Mrs. Irene McHenry and Mr.
Henry Schewell. The chore of typing the translations fell to
Mrs. Phyllis Moore and Mrs. Muriel Fuller. To all these
wonderful people, I express my sincere gratitude.

For their encouragement, guidance and constructive criti-
cism, I am indebted to members of the Board of Trustees of
the Santa Barbara Trust for Historic Preservation and its
staff, to Dr. Doyce B. Nunis, Jr., President of the Board of
Trustees of the Santa Barbara Mission Archive-Library, and
to the late Fr. Maynard Geiger who, until his death in 1977,
was Archivist at the Mission Archive-Library.

In addition to the acknowledgements for archival sources
in the notes and other places in the book, I wish to thank The
Bancroft Library, especially Miss Irene Moran and Mrs.
Vivian Fisher, the Newberry Library in Chicago, the Hunt-

ington Library in San Marino, the Archivo General de la
Nación in Mexico City, the Archivo General de Indias in
Seville, Spain, the Smithsonian Institution and the Library
of Congress for their cooperation in providing documentary
material.

I would be remiss and unappreciative if I did not acknowledge my indebtedness to [the late] Russell A. Ruiz, former
board member and historian of the Santa Barbara Trust for
Historic Preservation, who began his research on the Santa
Barbara Presidio before I had ever heard of it and who has
made innumerable valuable contributions to the presidio
reconstruction project. I am afraid that many times I have
used information gleaned from discussions with him without
paying proper tribute to his superior knowledge and insight
concerning the presidio project. Belatedly, I correct this
omission.

Lastly, for making possible the financing of publication
costs of the first two books I edited, I want to thank Mrs. Jean
Storke Menzies through whose efforts a revolving fund was
created by a grant from the Thomas More Storke Fund of the
Santa Barbara Foundation. This fund has made possible a
series of publications by local nonprofit organizations which
otherwise would not have been printed.

For reasons that will become obvious after reading about
the vulnerability of the group of buildings constituting the
Santa Barbara Presidio and of the fort's garrison, one might
question the aptness of the title of this book. A "citadel" is
defined as a "stronghold," which implies impregnability, an
ability to withstand major attacks.

The Santa Barbara Presidio was never directly attacked,
nor was it ever the subject of a siege. Its garrison could not
have repelled any determined effort by Indians to annihilate
it, and its adobe walls would quickly have crumbled under
any attack by foreign forces with land-based artillery. Yet the

four presidios at San Diego, Monterey, San Francisco and Santa Barbara served the purpose of anchoring Spain's hold on the lands of Alta California and providing security against attack by hostile Indians and invasion by foreign powers. From that standpoint, the term "citadel" is appropriate.

The story of the first California presidio at Loreto, Baja California, and the four Alta California presidios has, regrettably, been neglected by historians. Hundreds of books and articles have described the mission program, but no in-depth account of the role of the presidios in Spain's colonization program for the two Californias, nor a definitive history of the construction and activities of the individual establishments, has been written. Yet frequent reference has been made to the importance of these arsenals, if they can be so characterized, in supporting the work of the missions and defending Spain's settlements along the Pacific Coast. One reason may be that the physical remains of the presidios virtually disappeared due to earthquakes, weather and neglect. By contrast, most of the mission structures have survived through maintenance, repair and reconstruction, and many are still active as churches or museums or both.

Presidios were not as glamorous or romantic as the missions, being the representation of civil and military control, whereas the missions represented the religious and educational functions of government. In general, documentation on the presidios is harder to find than for the missions, but we are fortunate in that a considerable amount of information concerning the Santa Barbara Presidio has survived.

The principal early California historians have provided basic information in describing the course of events affecting the presidios during the period 1769 to 1850. Hubert Howe Bancroft, Zoeth Skinner Eldredge and Theodore H. Hittell have each written volumes on the history of California, and each preserved for posterity priceless documents invaluable

in reconstructing events and details of how they happened.[2]
Bancroft's monumental work, done between 1870 and 1890,
resulted in the collection now housed at The Bancroft
Library in Berkeley, California.

Local histories contain references to the presidio and mission period. For Santa Barbara, there are the writings of Fr.
Juan Caballería y Collel, Walter A. Hawley, Jesse D. Mason,
Charles M. Gidney, Michael J. Phillips, Yda Addis Storke
and Owen H. O'Neill, all written between 1872 and 1930.[3]
Often their information is taken from secondary sources for
the early period, and their reliability must be checked against
primary sources.

Because of the close relationship between the presidios
and the missions, the former are frequently mentioned in the
writings of the early missionaries, particularly Serra, Lasuén,
Payeras and Señán. These and other documents, such as the
baptismal, marriage and death registers on file at the Santa
Barbara Mission Archive-Library, provide valuable insights
into the life of the presidio garrison and the soldiers' families.

Foreigners visiting the Pacific Coast usually paid courtesy
calls on the commanding officers of the presidios in addition
to visiting the missions. Sometimes they described the establishments in their diaries, ship's logs or reports to their gov-
ernments. In some cases they gave fairly detailed accounts of
the strengths and weaknesses of the Spanish defenses, and
their observations add to our knowledge of the status of the
presidio as of the date of their visit.

By far the most valuable sources of information are the let-

---

[2]Bancroft, *History of California;* Eldredge, (ed.), *History of California;* and Hittell, *History of California.*

[3]Caballería y Collel, *History of the City of Santa Barbara;* Hawley, *The Early Days of Santa Barbara;* Mason (ed.), *History of Santa Barbara County;* Gidney, Brooks and Sheridan, *History of Santa Barbara, San Luis Obispo and Ventura Counties;* Phillips, *History of Santa Barbara County;* Storke, *A Memorial and Biographical History of the Counties of Santa Barbara, San Luis Obispo and Ventura;* and O'Neill (ed.), *History of Santa Barbara County.*

ters, reports, accounts and diaries found in the previously mentioned archives. The military and priestly dignitaries of the mission period were prolific letter writers. Because of the difficulties of travel, visits and inspections by their superiors were infrequent or nonexistent. Therefore regular and detailed reports and letters were required. Fortunately for posterity, many of these documents were preserved. The writer would laboriously make a copy of a letter or report for his record, and the recipient would often make a copy to be forwarded to higher authority. Thus a researcher may occasionally find as many as three copies of a document, not always identical because of omissions or errors in copying. Very important documents may bear the notation *Es Copia* and the signature of a person such as Antonio Bonilla, secretary to the commanding general of the *Provincias Internas,* or Internal Provinces, who was responsible for having the copy made and for certifying its validity.

The collection called the "Archives of California" at The Bancroft Library contains correspondence and reports of the presidio commanders. It provides more detailed information concerning the founding, construction and activities of the Santa Barbara Presidio than any other source so far consulted. Much of the material consists of summaries of the contents of the original document, and it is sometimes frustrating to see the words *sin importancia* at the end of a document that contains important details. Those words indicate that in the opinion of the scribe, but not necessarily of the present-day historian, the balance of the document was unimportant and so was not copied.

In addition to the Archives of California, The Bancroft Library also has microfilm reels containing much documentation from foreign archives. Neither these reels nor the archives themselves have been systematically searched for data on the California presidios. When finally someone is designated to research these sources for presidial information, some material in this book may have to be corrected.

The Santa Barbara Mission Archive-Library houses many documents pertaining to the presidio in the Junípero Serra Collection (JSC), the California Mission Document Collection (CMD) which incorporates the Alexander Taylor Collection, and the various subsections containing diaries and annual and biennial reports of the missions. For periods of a later date, the De la Guerra y Noriega Collection of family papers, many written by José de la Guerra y Noriega, fifth *comandante* of the Santa Barbara Presidio, is a useful resource. The Archive-Library has copies of the baptismal, marriage and death registers of most of the missions, a valuable source of information on the presidio soldiers and their families, as well as occasional data on the presidio buildings.

Other sources are the *Archivo General de Simancas* in Spain for the service records of soldiers, the Library of Congress and Smithsonian Institution, both in Washington D.C., Newberry Library in Chicago, Huntington Library in San Marino and the Honnold Library in Pomona. Maximum effort has been exerted to utilize original documents from the sources cited above. However, some problems exist:

    1. The Archives of California contain copies or summaries of original documents which were later destroyed in the 1906 San Francisco fire. All of Hubert H. Bancroft's employees were not necessarily experts. They were directed to examine papers in the various archives extant during the 1870s, copying or summarizing those considered of interest to Bancroft, and interviewing "old-timers" to record their reminiscences. These research assistants, like all of us, were fallible and may have made copying errors or may not have been expert in reading Spanish, the language in which most of the documents

were written. The people they interviewed may have had faulty memories or may have deliberately misled the interviewer to dramatize their importance.

2. The original documents themselves may have contained errors, either through ignorance or lack of education of the writer. Improper spelling could lead to inaccurate translation.

3. Accuracy of translation depends much on the knowledge and experience of the translator and his ability to interpret words in the context of the historical setting.

4. In describing the physical structure of presidio buildings, this author has had to rely on some conjecture based on the findings of the archaeological excavations at the Santa Barbara Presidio, or on what was found to exist at other presidios, missions or adobe buildings of the period, or on what appeared to the author to be logical and sensible. In each case the basis for the conclusion will be noted so that the reader can differ with the author if he wishes.

Every effort has been made to check the facts by comparison with the work of other writers on the same subjects, particularly those using the same source material, and to document the source and indicate whether or not the statements are conjectural or factual.

Because Bancroft's is the most authoritative compilation of information on the mission-presidio period, a detailed reading of his seven-volume *History of California* was the first step in the research for this study. Subsequently, the acquisition, compiling, indexing and translating of the documents used in this book have taken place over a period of more than twelve years. Translations were filed in chronological order and a notation made on each as to its source, date, writer, recipient and name of translator. It was early found that those archives contained many documents related to the presidios that were not listed in the notes. This necessitated several visits to The Bancroft Library and borrowing of reels of microfilmed documentation through interlibrary loan.

Whenever appropriate, material relating to presidios other than Santa Barbara was also copied, as well as material on the missions of San Buenaventura, Santa Inés, La Purísima, San Fernando and San Luis Obispo, the missions most closely related to the Santa Barbara Presidio. No effort was made to list documents specifically related to the Loreto, San Diego, Monterey or San Francisco presidios, although considerable data on them were included in the documents on Santa Barbara as a by-product. If in the future some historian decides to write comparable histories on the other presidios, the references compiled for the Santa Barbara Presidio should be consulted to avoid duplication of time and effort.

Many other books, articles, reports and documents were consulted and used in producing this book. Some, such as the reports of explorers and early visitors to Santa Barbara, provided information significant in describing the appearance of the presidio and the life of its inhabitants. Others, such as the logs of ships that anchored in Santa Barbara Bay prior to the 1850s, were disappointingly barren of useful data. This was particularly true of the logs of ships captained by the Yankee traders who visited the presidio but whose recorded descriptions were limited to the sharp financial deals they had arranged with the presidio officers. Finally, what has been presented in this book should be considered only as a start on an authoritative history of the Santa Barbara Presidio, one to be questioned and corrected as new facts are made available.

RICHARD S. WHITEHEAD

Chapter One

Alta California

Pageantry, religious rites and the beginning of much physical labor marked the mid-April day in 1782 when Spanish occupation of the Santa Barbara Channel coast began. It was a day of both fulfillment and commencement—it marked the end of much planning and advance preparation toward realization of long-delayed dreams, as well as the beginning of months of toil to bring forth what was considered an indispensable unit in California's occupation. But what chain of events brought about this late colonial period effort on Spain's far northern frontier?

Most Americans are somewhat aware of the hardships suffered by the explorers and early settlers of North America, the primitive housing, shortages of food supplies, lack of equipment and tools with which to perform simple tasks, hazards of wild animals and hostile natives, and isolation from the amenities of civilized areas. It is sometimes difficult to realize the effects of isolation, because we are not familiar with how knowledgeable the people who lived during that period were. For example, what construction tools did the soldiers who founded Santa Barbara have with which to erect their buildings? Did they have shovels, levels, hammers, a brace and bit? Did they measure with tapes? Did they have alarm clocks? How long did it take to load a musket? What medicines did they have? Did they have books that would tell them how to farm, how to cure sick people, how to construct buildings and how to make paper or glass? And how close to that norm was life in a newly-founded frontier province such as California?

A condensed chronology of Spain's achievements in colonizing North America will help in understanding some of the limitations and difficulties faced by soldiers and settlers in California. Columbus's discoveries were almost 300 years old, while 250 years had passed since Cortes's conquest of the Aztec empire. Yet both had a bearing on the founding of Santa Barbara, for that event was a distant lineal descendant of the epic activities of the Discoverer and the Conqueror. The sequence of historical events included, though was in no way restricted to, the discovery of Lower California in 1533; the wanderings of Alvar Núñez Cabeza de Vaca in the interior of North America; the first discovery of the California coast including a probable glimpse of the future site of Santa Barbara by Juan Rodríguez Cabrillo in 1542; the discovery of a return route from the Philippines for commercial vessels in the Spanish oriental trade, with the return voyage often passing the Channel Islands; and the detailed exploration of the California coast by Sebastián Vizcaíno's expedition of 1602-1603.

Elsewhere, northward advance in the interior of New Spain, as Mexico was then called, followed from mineral area to mineral area and brought with it creation of the first presidios, small forts manned by a handful of soldiers deployed to protect settlers, miners, and bullion. Expansion and Indian control were also entrusted to Catholic missionaries, who established missions supported by army troops when needed. The two basic institutions, the mission and the presidio, were complementary though not always harmonious in their relationship. Of the missionaries, the Jesuits had taken the lead in Spanish advance toward Alta California, only to suffer expulsion nearly on the eve of its occupation, resulting in Franciscans being sent instead.

Finally, the perceived threat of foreign encroachment on Spain's far-reaching empire, particularly the possibility of a Pacific Ocean challenge, led in 1768 and 1769 to a bold unprecedented plan to occupy physically the long-claimed land of Alta California, an area little known in any detail. Both England and Russia were thought to have designs on the coast.[1]

These evident threats to block the northward expansion of the Spanish empire in North America led high-ranking royal official José de Gálvez to take action to safeguard Spain's previously established claims to Alta California. As a competent planner, he realized the logistical problem and the need for a naval base to supply troops and settlers to the outpost area. He chose the estuary at the village of San Blas on the west coast of Mexico's mainland about sixty-five miles north of the present resort city of Puerto Vallarta as a ship-building yard and supply base, creating the Department of San Blas to operate it.[2] The site was subject to heavy rains and high temperatures, and swamps in the vicinity bred swarms of insects that carried disease and death to the soldiers, sailors and workmen in the port. Despite these liabilities, it functioned as an arsenal-shipyard and as the primary supply base for Alta California missions, presidios and pueblos for the next thirty-five years. It was from this base that the next operation contributing to establishment of the Santa Barbara Presidio was launched.

Planning for the colonizing expedition to Alta California, later to be called the "Sacred Expedition," was completed in 1768 by Gálvez, Viceroy Carlos de Croix and Fr. Junípero Serra. The ideal route would have been northward by land from Mexico City through Sinaloa and Sonora to the vicinity

---

[1] Text from the beginning of the chapter to this point is a summary by Donald Cutter of lengthier text in the original manuscript. Original manuscript available at the Presidio Research Center, Santa Barbara, California. *Ed. note.*

[2] Thurman, *The Naval Department of San Blas*, pp. 13-72.

of the junction of the Gila and Colorado rivers, thence westward via what is now El Centro to San Diego. This route was
impractical, however, because the Seri and Pima tribes were
waging war against the settlers of Sonora and because of the
intervening hostile terrain. Besides, an expedition by sea
would permit transportation of supplies more easily than by
muleback.

The temporary expedient, therefore, was two expeditions
by land and two by sea. The entire operation was commanded by Don Gaspar de Portolá who had been appointed
governor of the two Californias in November 1767. Fr.
Junípero Serra, newly-appointed president of the to-be-
established missions of Alta California, was placed in charge
of the religious aspects of the venture. The initial plan was to
occupy San Diego and Monterey with a presidio and a mission, and to establish a mission at some undetermined
halfway point to be called San Buenaventura.[3]

The sea expedition, involving the vessels *San Carlos* and
San Antonio, alias *El Príncipe*, embarked from San Blas September 26, 1768. A third vessel, the *San José*, was lost at sea.
Normally the voyage across the lower end of the Gulf of California required some fifteen to twenty days. The *San Carlos*
arrived at La Paz in Baja California on December 25th, taking aboard six inches of water per hour, its tackle and rigging
in shreds, its cargo badly damaged and its crew without fresh
provisions. Within fifteen days, Gálvez, who had taken
another ship to La Paz, supervised the refitting of the ship
and it was ready for sea in early January of 1769. The *San
Antonio* also suffered damage, though not as badly, and it was
likewise made ready for sea in about three weeks.

The latter ship, a packetboat, had been built to facilitate

---

[3]Chapman, *The Founding of Spanish California, 1687-1783*, pp. 68-129; Richman, *California Under Spain and Mexico*, pp. 62-89; and Geiger, (trans.), *Palóu's Life of Fray Junípero
Serra*, pp. 53-69.

transport for the Sonora war against the Indians. The *San Carlos*, also a packetboat, left La Paz in Baja California on January 9, 1769, with sixty-two men on board. The *San Antonio* left Cape San Lucas on February 15th. The ill-fated *San José* was dispatched from Loreto on June 16th to an unknown end.

The first land expedition, under Captain Fernando de Rivera y Moncada, with twenty-five soldiers, three muleteers and forty-two Christian Indians, marched northward up the Baja California peninsula to Santa María de los Angeles, one of the northern Baja California missions. Along the way it picked up livestock and church supplies at various missions as a means of reducing overall costs. Fr. Juan Crespí, who wrote the most complete diary of the journey, joined the party at Velicatá. The cavalcade departed from there for San Diego on March 24, 1769.

The second land expedition left Loreto on March 6th under the command of Governor Portolá. Fr. Serra was in this party, along with a dozen soldiers and servants and forty-four Baja California natives. The two ships and the two land parties arrived at San Diego between April 29th and June 28th. Of the three hundred men who had left Mexico, including those on the *San José*, only half reached San Diego. About seventy-five had lost their lives to scurvy or other diseases and accidents.[4]

At San Diego, the soldiers repulsed efforts by the Indians to steal cloth, utensils and even pieces of the ship's sails. This led to a violent attack by the Indians with their bows and arrows, but since they had never heard the sound of gunfire before, they withdrew as soon as the soldiers began firing their muskets. One servant of the expedition was killed, as were several local Indians. Finally the Indians sought peace,

[4]Bolton, *Fray Juan Crespí*, pp. 122-165.

and brought their wounded to the expedition surgeon to be healed.

On July 16, 1769, Fr. Junípero Serra and the remaining soldiers established the Mission and Presidio of San Diego, taking possession of the land in the accustomed symbolic ceremony of pulling up grass, moving stones and breaking branches as visual proof of sovereignty. An announcement was made that the land was being claimed in the name of the King of Spain. This was followed by the raising of the cross, the blessing of the land and a solemn Mass.

The rite of taking possession was performed each time an explorer discovered new territory. It took various forms, but essentially consisted of four parts: the religious ceremony, the proclamation, the symbolic ritual and the formal attestation by a notary.[5] The proclamation was delivered verbally by the discoverer in command of the expedition and could be attested to by all present at the ceremony. In some cases, the record relates that possession was taken without protest by the natives. Since the Indians undoubtedly were totally ignorant of the significance of the ceremony, the record in this respect was somewhat superfluous, if not a farce. The symbolic actions of cutting trees, moving dirt and stones and throwing ocean water on the land were vestiges of medieval customs of Germanic origin. The attestation by a notary and the presence of witnesses were supposed to be added assurances that posterity and foreign countries would recognize the claim.

On July 14th, two days earlier, an expedition of sixty-four men under Portolá left to find the port of Monterey and to explore the coastline by land between the two ports. Men who were later to become important in the early history of California and of Santa Barbara accompanied the expedi-

---

[5]Servín, "Symbolic Acts of Sovereignty in Spanish California," pp. 255-67; and Kelsey, *Juan Rodríguez Cabrillo*, pp. 133-34.

tion. One of them was Sergeant José Francisco Ortega, who served as trailblazer and advance guard to search out on horseback the best route for the next day's journey. He later became the first *comandante* of the Santa Barbara Presidio. Pedro Fages, who became governor of the Californias from July 1782 to April 1791, and Fernando de Rivera y Moncada, who became Lieutenant Governor of Baja California and who was killed in the Yuma Indian uprising of 1781, were also on the expedition. Miguel Costansó, a trained military engineer, was in the party and later wrote critical reports on the presidios and other defenses of California. Fr. Juan Crespí, the principal priest and diarist of the trek, was on the lookout for good mission sites. All five wrote diaries of the trip, but Crespí's is the most detailed and informative.[6]

The Portolá expedition reached the present site of Ventura on August 14, 1769. Fr. Crespí was full of praise for that area as a site for a mission, ignoring what was later to be a primary consideration for a presidio site, the need for a safe anchorage for ships.

At Santa Barbara, where they arrived four days later on August 18th, Crespí wrote:

> With some difficulty we crossed a large estuary which penetrates deeply into the land, passed near the [Indian] village, and pitched camp about two gunshots [about 2000 feet] from it. Near the camp we found a large lagoon which does not seem to be seasonal, but to have a spring in the center. This town was called Laguna de la Concepción.[7]

The estuary Fr. Crespí mentions was the *estero* that shows up on early maps of the city and on U.S. Coast and Geodetic Survey maps (see figure 1).[8] It covered the area extending

---

[6]Bolton said of Crespí: "Among all the great diarists who recorded explorations in the New World, Juan Crespí occupied a conspicuous place." Bolton, *Crespí*, p. xiii.

[7]Bolton, *Crespí*, p. 165.

[8]U.S. Coast Survey, *Map of the Port of Santa Barbara, California*, Register No. 373, 1852.

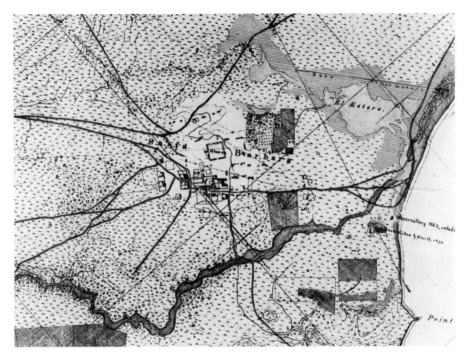

Figure 1: A portion of the 1852 United States Coast Survey
Map of Santa Barbara, California, 1852.

generally from Cabrillo Boulevard to Santa Barbara High
School and from Santa Barbara Street to Milpas Street
except for the ridges of land that create hills in the streets
within this area. The Indian village that Crespí called a town
was located on Burton Mound, a hill just inland from
Cabrillo Boulevard between Bath and Chapala streets, which
would later be the Potter Hotel site. The Indian village was
named *Syujtún*, pronounced Shuktu, and it was later the
object of an intensive archaeological investigation by John P.
Harrington.[9]

[9]Harrington, *Exploration of the Burton Mound at Santa Barbara, California*, pp. 23-168.

Evidently the expedition came along the beach from the east and camped somewhere in the vicinity of State and Figueroa streets. The lagoon or lake near which they camped and which inspired Crespí's name for Santa Barbara, Laguna de la Concepción, also shows on the early maps. It was centered at the intersection of what is now Laguna and Cota streets. One of the city wells, known as the De la Guerra well and presumably utilizing the spring in the lake mentioned by Crespí, is located at the southwest corner of Laguna and Ortega streets. This well once watered the De la Guerra Gardens maintained by José Antonio de la Guerra y Noriega, long-term *comandante* of the Santa Barbara Presidio.

Apparently Crespí was not much impressed by Santa Barbara because he failed to recommend it as a mission site. Neither did the military, at this time, see its advantages as a site for a presidio, but we can overlook their lack of discernment since they were not looking for presidio sites and were preoccupied with what lay ahead of them.

After leaving the site of the future City of Santa Barbara, the expedition proceeded westerly along the coast to Point Concepción, thence northwesterly to a point just north of Cambria, where the proximity of the rugged Santa Lucia Mountains crowding against the shore forced them to turn inland, eventually coming to the Salinas Valley. Following the Salinas River, they finally reached Monterey Bay, but failed to recognize it from Vizcaíno's ancient description. The main party remained in camp while the advance party under Sergeant Ortega continued northward and discovered San Francisco Bay, recognizing Point Reyes and the Farallon Islands from previous reports, but being the first white men to see the bay itself.

Weary, cold and on an almost starvation diet, the expedition returned to San Diego where, after consultation, they decided they had in fact found Monterey. A second land party under Portolá left San Diego in April 1770 for the same destination, but this time the *San Antonio*, having returned to San Blas, replenished its supplies and replaced its crew, also sailed northward. Arriving in May with Fr. Serra aboard, the group now identified the Monterey site and, on June 3, 1770, celebrated the founding of the Monterey Presidio and the Mission of San Carlos. At this mission, Fr. Serra established his headquarters for the California missions, while the center of operations for Fages as military commander was set up in the presidio.

In May 1771, ten priests from Mexico arrived at Monterey on the *San Antonio* together with all the furnishings to equip five new missions. Equipment for the mission honoring St. Bonaventure, the "Seraphic Doctor" who was a favorite of Fr. Serra, was already in storage at Monterey. Due in part to insufficient *escoltas* (soldiers assigned to protect, guard and assist the priests in their work of building missions), these priests were given responsibility for founding missions at San Gabriel, San Antonio and San Luis Obispo instead of San Buenaventura, which Serra had decided should be at the easterly entrance to the Santa Barbara Channel.[10] Concurrently, due to Serra's well-founded fear that the soldiers would corrupt the neophyte Indians if the presidios were side by side with the missions, he moved the San Carlos Mission from Monterey to Carmel. Partly for the same reason, San Diego Mission was moved to a location four miles up river from the San Diego Presidio.

Some hostilities with the natives were experienced during the founding of San Gabriel Mission in September 1771. As a result, when Fages arrived a few days later with soldiers to man the new Mission of San Buenaventura, he decided to postpone the founding and reinforce the guard at San

---

[10]Tibesar, *The Writings of Junípero Serra*, vol. I, pp. 197-209.

Gabriel.[11] This incident delayed a settlement on the Santa Barbara Channel for more than ten years.

A year later, Fr. Serra traveled from Monterey to San Diego with Fages and a contingent of soldiers, and along the way founded San Luis Obispo Mission on September 1, 1772. There he left a priest, five soldiers and two Christian Indians to construct the mission. Continuing south, the party was attacked by hostile Indians at the Rincón, about three miles east of Carpinteria. According to Father Serra, one man was killed and another left dying. Apparently the struggle developed from an attempted theft.[12] Arriving at the location of the present City of Ventura, Serra reconnoitered the area and decided on the present site of the San Buenaventura Mission.[13]

Fr. Serra once again asked Commander Fages for enough soldiers to establish the San Buenaventura Mission. Because of the isolation and the hostility of the Indians, he suggested the *escolta* consist of at least twenty soldiers.[14] Fages again refused, probably precipitating the feud between the two which resulted in Serra's trip to Mexico a few months later.[15] As a result of Serra's presentation to the Viceroy and others, Fages was removed as military commander in August of 1774.[16] These incidents will be discussed in more detail in the next chapter.

In October 1774, Felipe de Neve, who had distinguished himself as a diplomatic administrator when assigned to the duty of expelling the Jesuit order from Mexico in 1767 and managing their properties until 1774, was appointed governor of the two Californias. He succeeded Felipe Barri, who

[11]Geiger, *The Life and Times of Junípero Serra*, vol. I, pp. 304-08.

[12]Geiger, *Life and Times of Serra*, I, 325.

[13]Geiger, *Life and Times of Serra*, I, 325.

[14]Tibesar, *Writings of Serra*, I, 273.

[15]Bancroft, *California*, I, 207-13.   [16]Bancroft, *California*, I, 215.

had filled the position for five years. Neve spent a little less than two years at the capital at the presidio of Loreto in Baja California, then was directed to move the capital to Monterey and take personal charge of the affairs of Alta California. Rivera y Moncada was to be sub-governor at Loreto.[17]

In July 1775, Fr. Serra wrote to Fr. Francisco Pangua, Guardian of the Franciscan College of San Fernando in Mexico City. Regarding the jeopardy of Spaniards in the narrow plain between Point Concepción and Ventura, Serra claimed that the Santa Barbara Channel is "what calls most urgently for attention, before the whole countryside breaks out into war; and it would be only by sheer force of arms that one could make any headway there, even just to pass through it."[18] He described a confrontation at the place called Dos Pueblos (the two Indian villages on either side of Dos Pueblos Creek eight miles west of the present-day town of Goleta, which were called San Pedro and San Pablo by the Spanish and *Mikiw* and *Cuyam* by the Indians):

> One of the soldiers saw fit to cuff a gentile [a non-Christian Indian] who, from curiosity, had tried to take his rifle. All of them took up their arms; arrows flew everywhere and six gentiles were killed by the soldiers.[19]

In describing the same incident, Father Fermín Francisco de Lasuén, then stationed at Monterey with Fr. Serra, stated that the Indian cut off the tail of the soldier's mule and tried to disarm him. When the melee occurred, Lasuén, who had dismounted to give beads to the Indian children, took off on foot, a move that he described as difficult because he was a corpulent man. His actions could be considered comical had it not been such a hazardous situation.[20]

[17]Beilharz, *Felipe de Neve: First Governor of California*, pp. 13-16.

[18]Tibesar, *Writings of Serra*, II, 289-97.

[19]Tibesar, *Writings of Serra*, II, 295.

[20]Kenneally, *Writings of Lasuén*, 1965), vol. I, p. 46.

Lasuén further commented:

> It is a matter of deep regret that by deferring the founding of a mission in that region [the Santa Barbara Channel], which manifestly offers many sites that are suitable for that purpose and conveniently located for the natives, many of them will suffer in the continual wars which they wage among themselves, as the signs of their attacks and manifest evidences of their destruction indicate.
>
> Furthermore, due to this delay in establishing a mission, the Indians are becoming bolder...[and] there is danger that in time the conversion of these Indians will be rendered more difficult and more costly. These Channel Indians know that they are strong, and they act on the principle that whoever harms them will have to pay the price.[21]

Meantime, the project to establish a direct land route between Sonora and Alta California had not been forgotten. As long as the settlements along the coast were dependent on transport by sea for their supplies, their support in case of attack was extremely weak and their isolation dangerous. Under date of September 10, 1772, a regulation had been issued by the King setting forth instructions for operation of presidios forming a line of defense generally along the northern boundary of Mexico.[22]

Father Serra, absent from Alta California on his trip to Mexico City from September 1772 to mid-March 1774, learned that the Viceroy planned to abandon the San Blas establishment in order to reduce expenses in accord with the 1772 regulations. Serra's strong opposition to this proposal led to publication of another *Reglamento* dated May 19, 1773, called the "Echeveste Regulations," which perpetuated operation of the San Blas supply depot and improved its service to the missions and presidios. These regulations, along with one prepared by Governor Neve dated October 24, 1781, will be discussed in more detail in the next chapter.

---

[21]Kenneally, *Writings of Lasuén*, I, 45-47.
[22]Brinckerhoff and Faulk, *Lancers for the King*, pp. 11-67.

In Serra's list of thirty-two suggestions for improvements in the government of the Alta California missions dated March 13, 1773, most of which were approved, Serra recommended that Captain Juan Bautista de Anza of the Tubac Presidio, in what is now southern Arizona, be authorized to undertake an expedition to discover a land route from northern Mexico to San Diego or Monterey.[23] With this support, Anza's request for authorization to conduct the expedition was approved, and he set out on the journey from Tubac on January 8, 1774. His cavalcade of twenty soldiers, driving sixty head of cattle, suffered many hardships crossing the Colorado Desert, but finally arrived at Mission San Gabriel just over ten weeks later. Thus the land route was scouted. In October 1775, Anza made another trip from Tubac to San Gabriel, this time taking sixteen weeks, partly because there were in the party 165 mules, 340 horses and 320 head of cattle, plus 235 people, most of whom were to remain in California.[24]

From San Gabriel, Anza traveled to San Diego to provide support for Lieutenant José Francisco Ortega, who had been in command of the San Diego Presidio since 1773 but was having trouble with hostile Indians. From there, Anza marched north to Monterey and San Francisco where he delivered the new settlers safely and then returned to Tubac. On September 17, 1776, a little more than three months after the American Continental Congress approved the Declaration of Independence, the Presidio of San Francisco was founded.[25]

On Sunday, February 26, 1776, Anza and his colonists passed through Santa Barbara, and Fr. Pedro Font, diarist of the expedition, wrote a detailed description of the Chumash Indians and their way of life. He also wrote:

---

[23]Tibesar, *Writings of Serra*, I, 295-327.
[24]Bancroft, *California*, I, 258-59.
[25]Bancroft, *California*, I, 286-89.

In all this coast, although there are more than thirty arroyos, there is no place to establish a good mission because of the small amount of water which the arroyos carry, for many dry up in the course of the year, and especially for lack of sufficient level lands suitable for crops, although pasturage is plentiful and good in all places and in some places there is an abundance of timber and trees.[26]

However, the following day he recorded:

At a league we came to Mescaltitán, a pretty place which appeared to be a good site for a mission. Here there are three large [Indian] villages, two somewhat apart on the banks of the estuary, the largest one on the road which we are traveling.[27]

Mescaltitán was the name given the Goleta Slough area by the soldiers of the Portolá expedition in 1769 because of its similarity to a lake with an island in the middle bearing that name and located on the west coast of Mexico about 140 miles north of Puerto Vallarta. The hill on which the Goleta sewage plant is now located was, in the eighteenth and nineteenth centuries, an island surrounded by water to a depth of twelve feet. In August 1782, Juan Pantoja y Arriaga, second pilot of the frigate *Princesa*, mapped this area and the Bay of Santa Barbara when his ship, the first to anchor at Santa Barbara, brought supplies to the new presidio.[28]

The Indian village on Anza's route through the area was called *Saspili* and was located at the Fairview Avenue overpass over U.S. Highway 101. On the hill in the middle of the slough was the village of *Helo*, capital of all the villages in the Goleta area. In 1941, the top of this hill was graded down to provide fill to create the Santa Barbara Airport. The hill is still shown as Mescaltitan Island on the U.S. Geological Survey map for the Goleta quadrangle.

---

[26]Bolton, *Font's Diary*, p. 256.

[27]Bolton, *Font's Diary*, p. 260.

[28]For the Santa Barbara portion of Pantoja's log see: Sahyun (trans.) and Whitehead (ed.), *The Voyage of the Frigate Princesa*, pp. 63-70.

Thus the stage was set for the settlement of Santa Barbara and establishment of its presidio. Between 1767 and January of 1777, the supply base at San Blas had been established and two ships built there, and missions had been founded at San Diego, Carmel, San Antonio, San Gabriel, San Luis Obispo, San Juan Capistrano and Santa Clara. A land route had been explored from Sonora to the California settlements and a start had been made toward a settlement at San Francisco. No major catastrophe had befallen the settlers and soldiers, and with some exceptions, harmony existed between them and the natives.

Chapter Two

Reglamentos

Expansion of the settlement of colonial New Spain from Mexico City northward had been severely hampered by opposition of the native Indians of Northern Mexico, first the Chichimecas and later the Apaches. A considerable number of presidios had been built and manned to protect the priests, miners and settlers, but the hostile tribes were effectively complicating development in the provinces of Sinaloa, Nueva Vizcaya, Sonora, New Mexico, Coahuila, and Texas, called the *Provincias Internas* or Internal Provinces. Because of their distance from Mexico City, control of military groups fighting the Indians was difficult. Furthermore, there was no overall plan for defense of the Internal Provinces.

The frontier problem was assigned by Visitor General José de Gálvez to the Marqués de Rubí who, with a trained military engineer, Nicolás de Lafora, surveyed the entire region between 1766 and 1768. Together they presented a plan for a cordon of presidios stretching from the Gulf of California to the Gulf of Mexico, generally along what is now the southern boundary of the United States.[1] Concurrently, José de Gálvez made a tour of some of the same area and recommended a major change in the administration of the territory. The result of the Rubí and Gálvez reports was issuance of the *Reglamento e instrucción para los presidios que se han de formar*

---

[1]Brinckerhoff and Faulk, *Lancers*, pp. 49-67, plus map opposite p. 80.

en la línea de frontera de la Nueva España approved by the King in September of 1772.

These Royal Regulations of 1772, as subsequently modified, were an effective system, evidenced by the fact that they were the basis for defense from 1772 through the Independence of Mexico and until 1848. The Regulations have been translated in a book entitled *Lancers for the King*, which also contains drawings of presidio soldiers and descriptions of their weapons and equipment, together with a map showing the locations of the presidios in northern Mexico.[2] There are fourteen titles or sections, each devoted to some facet of military administration of the area, with slight reference to California, all signed *"Yo, El Rey"* (I, the King).

In brief, the Regulations, primarily applicable to the presidios along the northern border of Mexico, established the following:

1. The earlier practice of paying soldiers in merchandise sold to them at excessive prices was forbidden and commanders of garrisons were prohibited from participating in the purchase of provisions and equipment for the garrisons. Payments to troops and purchases of goods were assigned to an *habilitado* or paymaster chosen from among the members of the company. He received two percent of each soldier's pay for the duty of keeping accounts and making purchases for the company.

2. The presidio complements of officers and soldiers were set out with their pay scales, which ranged from annual salaries of 3000 *pesos* for the captain, 700 *pesos* for a lieutenant, 500 *pesos* for an ensign or second lieutenant, 480 for a chaplain, 350 for a sergeant, 300 for each of two corporals, 3 *reales* (8 *reales* = 1 *peso*) per day for each of ten Indian scouts and 290 *pesos* per year for each of 43 to 77 privates, depending on the location of the presidio. In addition to their pay, a gratuity of ten *pesos* per year was paid to each soldier from the common fund.

3. The regulations prescribed the uniform and equipment of the presidial soldiers, consisting of a short jacket of blue woolen cloth

---

[2]Brinckerhoff and Faulk, *Lancers*, pp. 1-67.

with small cuffs and a red collar, breeches of blue wool, a blue cloth cap, a leather jacket (from which these soldiers received the name of *soldados de cuera*), a cartridge pouch, bandoleer embroidered with the name of the presidio, black neckerchief, hat, shoes and leggings. The weapons were a broad sword, lance, shield made of several layers of leather, musket, and a pair of pistols, each of which were described in detail. Responsibility for keeping his weapons clean and serviceable rested with the soldier, assisted by an armorer who maintained a reserve supply of arms. Each soldier was to have six horses, one colt and one mule. One horse was to be kept saddled and tethered at all times, ready for immediate duty. The cost of uniforms, arms, equipment and mounts was paid by the soldier. Corporals and privates were paid two *reales* per day in cash for the personal expenses of themselves and their families, and twenty to twenty-five *pesos* per year were withheld for their retirement and the welfare of their families. Replacement of lost or worn out clothing, equipment and horses came out of the soldier's income. Upon his discharge or death, the soldier's military belongings were sold and the money given to him or his heirs or used to pay off any debts.

4. The soldier could buy food, clothing and other items for himself and his family from the company supply store or from visiting merchants, but obviously in an outpost like Santa Barbara few merchants visited.

5. Three pounds of gunpowder distributed in cartridges, with bullets, were allocated annually to each soldier. An extra three pounds were allotted during the first year of service because of the necessity for more frequent target practice.

6. Maintenance of detailed records of pay, soldiers' service time, performance, vacancies, supplies, allowances, promotions and unusual events were mandatory, and those voluminous records that survive provide boring but revealing information on presidio operations. Failure of officers to keep complete and honest records of this nature was grounds for a dishonorable discharge and two years imprisonment.

7. Title Ten stipulated that the King's main goal was the welfare and conversion of the gentile (as contrasted with the Christianized) Indians and the tranquility of the frontier. Active war was to be waged against the hostile Indians, but prisoners were to be sent to the vicinity of Mexico City, and any soldier found guilty of killing

an Indian in cold blood was to be sentenced to death. Nevertheless, the regulations warned against clemency for the Apaches who were known for professing a desire for peace, then interpreting kind treatment as weakness, escaping, and killing their former captors. Slavery of Indians was prohibited.

8. Settlement of the area by immigrants and retired soldiers and their families was to be encouraged by allotment of land to them by the presidio commander.

9. The office of Commanding General of the Interior Provinces was created with jurisdiction over all the presidios and their garrisons and over their internal and military operations. This provision was effectuated by appointment of Teodoro de Croix, nephew of the Viceroy, as Commanding General with headquarters at Arizpe, about 150 miles south of Tucson, Arizona. Croix was to have all the powers of the Viceroy except those related to supplies, which obviously had to originate in Mexico City. The functions and responsibilities of all officers, non-commissioned officers and privates were also delineated, with particular detail to the position of paymaster. This position was filled every three years by vote of the subaltern officers, the chaplain, and a representative of the soldiers, either a sergeant, corporal or a private.

10. Lastly, the Regulations relocated many of the presidios to form a cordon of fifteen fortresses at intervals of about forty miles stretching from the Gulf of California to the Gulf of Mexico. Almost as an afterthought, these regulations were applied to the presidios of the Californias.

When these regulations were approved there were in Alta California the five missions at San Diego, Carmel, San Antonio, San Gabriel and San Luis Obispo plus the two presidios of San Diego and Monterey. There was also a distant presidio at Loreto, Baja California. Father Junípero Serra, President of the Alta California missions, was preparing for a trip to Mexico City to present a number of complaints to the viceroy.

Among thirty-two of Serra's written grievances was a request that Military Commander Fages be replaced.[3] Serra

---

[3]Tibesar, *Writings of Serra*, I, 295-327.

recommended Sergeant José Francisco Ortega, later to become the first *comandante* of the Santa Barbara Presidio, as Fages's replacement. Fages had held the position since 1770 when Portolá returned to Mexico. Fr. Serra accused Fages of meddling in the discipline of neophyte Indians, of withholding and opening private mail of the missionaries, and of diverting mission supplies. His worst offense, according to Serra, was failure to punish soldiers for illicit relations with Indian women, resulting not only in neutralizing the moral teachings of the padres but also of accelerating the spread of venereal disease among the Indians. Serra also asked that the missionaries be given full control over the management, education and punishment of the baptized natives, except for crimes of blood.

One other request by Serra was that plans to close the supply depot at San Blas and replace the annual supply ships with land caravans be abandoned. He argued that the proposal to supply the missions overland from the southeast or from the south would require 1500 mules and 100 guards and muleteers.[4]

Serra was successful in most of his entreaties. The Council of War and Royal Treasury approved twenty-two of his requests. The friars were given full control over the mission Indians, and they were allowed to send back to the presidio any soldier of the guard without indicating their reason for the action. Mail and freight were to be delivered to them directly without passing through the hands of the governor, and they were given free mail privileges. The San Blas operations were continued and Fages was recalled to Mexico City in August 1773.[5]

One result of Serra's pleading was the so-called "Echeveste Regulations," developed by Juan José de Echeveste for the

---

[4]Tibesar, *Writings of Serra*, I, 331-43.
[5]Bancroft, *California*, I, 207-16.

viceroy, dated May 19, 1773, and becoming effective January 1, 1774.[6] This document referred primarily to the number of troops to be stationed at the various presidios and missions, their salaries, the personnel and salaries involved in the operation of the Naval Department of San Blas, including the shipyard and the ships' crews, and general items of a financial nature. It did assure continuance of the mission supply system by the sea route.

Felipe de Neve was appointed Governor of the Californias in October 1774.[7] In 1775, the King ordered a new *reglamento* because of defects in the previous regulations and slow progress in settling Alta California. Viceroy Antonio María Bucareli assigned this task to Commanding General Croix who, in August of 1777, reassigned it to Neve as the person most familiar with the problems and most competent to develop solutions.[8] Neve used the Regulations of 1772 for his basic outline and submitted a new set of regulations to Croix in June of 1779. Croix approved Neve's draft without change and forwarded it to the new viceroy, Martín de Mayorga, with the recommendation that it be put into effect on an interim basis pending approval by the King. With approval of the King on October 24, 1781, the Neve Regulation became law.

Neve's *Regulations for Governing the Province of the Californias* applied to the presidios of Alta and Baja California, to the Department of San Blas and, to a certain extent, to the California missions.[9] These regulations detailed many changes in the financial transactions affecting the presidios and their garrisons, including sale to the presidios of crops grown by the pueblos and the provision of mules to carry the

[6]Bolton (trans.), *Palóu's Historical Memoirs* vol. III, pp. 37-128.
[7]Beilharz, *Neve*, p. 13.
[8]Beilharz, *Neve*, p. 13.
[9]Johnson (trans), *Regulations for Governing the Province of the Californias*, pp. 9-49

cargos; support of two master mechanics, a carpenter and three blacksmiths at Monterey and San Diego; and increases in the salaries of officers and soldiers.

Specific references in these regulations to the planned settlement at Santa Barbara included:

> The Channel of Santa Barbara is distant seventy-four leagues [195 miles] from the presidio of San Diego and seventy [184 miles] from that of Monterey. It extends about twenty-six leagues [68 miles] between the coast and the *Sierra de la Cieneguilla,* its greatest width being half to three-quarters of a league [2 miles].[10] The pass is full of high hills, ravines and deep fissures where it is estimated from eight to ten thousand heathen live occupying twenty-one populous *rancherías* [Indian villages] which are situated at short distances from each other on the heights and headlands contiguous to the shore. The *Camino Real* runs very close to the shore, when not actually on it, or on the heights.[11] This evidences the dangers to which small squads traversing it are exposed and if some incident causes ill will or open enmity on the part of the heathen, the means of communication between the old and the new establishments would be cut off. Because of these urgent reasons, it has been determined to occupy the pass in the following manner.
>
> The presidio, which must be located at the center of the Channel, shall be composed of a company consisting of a lieutenant, one *alférez* and twenty-nine soldiers, including one sergeant and two corporals. Under its shelter a mission shall be established which later shall be moved to the nearest spot affording more land and water sufficient for farming, at which time the garrison shall supply it with an escort of one corporal and five soldiers. For its complete occupation, two other reductions shall be founded at either end of said Channel, each to be garrisoned with one sergeant and fourteen soldiers. These troops shall be considered as supernumerary to the company at the presidio until such time as these establishments are

---

[10]The regulations here refer to the shelf of the mainland between Ventura and Point Conception, then called the Pass of Santa Barbara. The Sierra de la Cieneguilla refers to the Santa Ynez Mountains, the backdrop of the Santa Barbara plain, so-called because of the marshy area (*ciénaga*) at Goleta, now the site of the Santa Barbara Airport.

[11]The *Camino Real* is not "The King's Highway" as some interpret it, but the main or commonly traveled road. For an excellent treatment of the subject see: J.N. Bowman, "The Roads of Provincial California,"

sure of peace and the good will of the heathen. When the hoped-for rapid progress is made in the spiritual conquest, they shall be proportionately reduced until they consist of the usual escort of one corporal and five soldiers each. The sergeants shall be sent to increase the companies at San Diego and Monterey, and the sixteen remaining soldiers shall be appointed to garrison other reductions which it may be decided to found, in which case they shall be annexed to the companies nearest the sites selected.

The annual allowance of the presidio to be established at the Channel of Santa Barbara shall be 7,577 *pesos*, 4 *reales*, to which shall be added 6,895 *pesos*, the corresponding amount for the two escorts temporarily provided, making a total of 14,472 *pesos*, 4 *reales*.

The document then lists the increased salaries of the members of the garrison.

Until this regulation became law, the soldiers apparently were receiving uniforms fitted to only one size, because it orders that the paymasters henceforth order uniforms made in proportionate sizes and to individual measure. Horses were to be pastured in the environs of the presidios and brought in daily, morning and night, "but the established practice of keeping four horses by day and eight by night tied in the presidio must not be altered."

The gratuity fund of the presidio, at the rate of ten *pesos* per private soldier, was designated for meeting the cost of rations for Indian prisoners and those who came to arrange a truce, and for maintenance of the muleteers, pack saddles and pack mules which were provided for the benefit of the company as a whole. The text of the regulations continues:

As it is inevitable that there will be damage to grain and articles of food after they are received, chiefly in the case of *maize* [corn], which is commonly landed wormy, and lard and *panocha* [crude brown cane sugar], which the heat in the holds of the vessels melts and ferments, the latter remaining fermented—the fogs and humidity of this climate even causing it to dissolve—to which losses must be added the shrinkage and waste caused by retailing and in the conveyance of these articles and provisions necessary for the subsistence of the troops acting as escorts, the paymaster should not report these losses, nor also in the case of fabrics whose measure does not correspond with its respective measurement at retail, it being proper that the common fund suffer these losses. The paymaster shall be liable for preventable shortages and shrinkages as well as those which result from carelessness in sorting and guarding whatever is entrusted to his care.

The stock of powder and shot held at each presidio should amount to sixteen pounds per soldier in view of the difficulty and risks attending their shipment from Mexico. Candidates [for vacant positions of sergeant] must be chosen from among those who have most distinguished themselves through their conduct and valor, taking care as much as possible that they know how to read and write, and the Governor shall approve the one he thinks most suitable. Whenever any soldier shall die or be discharged, in view of the urgency of buying his mounts and equipment to supply the recruit taking his place, the paymaster shall take these articles...and distribute them at the same price at which he received them.

While paymasters are not to make expenditures to supply provisions, clothing and other articles, being bound to the costs, responsibility and safekeeping of general and private accounts of the troops and subordinates of the presidios, they shall deduct from the captain, officers, surgeon, sergeants, corporals, privates, and subordinates, two per cent as commission for their services and costs. Grants shall be made by the Governor in the name of His Majesty to those who come newly to settle, particularly to soldiers who by having served the time of their enlistment or because of advanced age are retired from the service, as also to the families of those who die.

The maize, beans, garbanzos, and lentils produced by the crops of the pueblos, after the citizens have reserved the amount necessary for their own subsistence and planting, shall be bought for the provision of the presidios and paid for in cash at the prices established.[12]

---

[12]Author Whitehead made a few minor changes for purposes of clarification of Johnson's original translation.

Chapter Three

Planning and Preparation

The first written statement that a fort was to be established at the Santa Barbara Channel appears in a letter written as early as March 1, 1777, by Father Junípero Serra to Viceroy Bucareli. Serra had made his third trip along the Santa Barbara Channel in December 1776, experiencing storms which forced travel along the high land instead of the easier route along the beach. Evidently the natives were very friendly, for Serra described how they linked arms with him to help him over the muddy, steep hills. He wrote:

> What a pleasure it is for me to see them, in great numbers, walking along the road with me, and breaking out into song each time I started a tune for them to take up. When the first batch took its leave, a second group, watching out for the opportunity, would come up for me to make the sign of the cross upon their foreheads. Some followed me many days. All of that, for me, added spurs to the feelings of pity which I have had for them these many years.
>
> But it gave me matter for considerable encouragement, too, when I heard from the Governor's [Neve's] own mouth, the statement that his own journey through the same territory [in January 1777] and the sight of the natives there, had impressed him how urgently important it was that they should be brought into our holy Catholic faith; that a fort, or presidio, should be established in the middle of the said Channel where ships may stop; that a mission should be near it, and two more at the two extremities [of the Channel]. San Buenaventura should be at one end, and Point La Concepción at the other. The fort at Santa Barbara would protect the whole channel. It would mean a considerable increase in numbers of Christians and subjects of the Crown; and, for all the new

establishments here, it would mean a most important advantage of a more secure passage. This plan, as proposed by the Governor, is so much in accord with my dreams of long ago that, when I heard it, in the midst of the joy it occasioned me, I recognized once more that right reason and truth are practically the same thing. Your Excellency will decide what seems to you to be for the best.[1]

Governor Felipe de Neve's report to the Viceroy, dated June 3, 1777, and incorporating his impressions of the Santa Barbara area, is even more informative. A royal order dated April 19, 1776, was forwarded by the Viceroy to Neve directing him to move the capital of the Californias from Loreto, Baja California, to Monterey, Alta California, and to take personal charge of the affairs of Alta California. Arriving at Monterey on February 3, 1777, he wrote:

On the trip which I made from San Diego to this presidio [of Monterey], I examined with particular attention the situation of the *rancherías* of the *Gentiles* [unconverted Indians] which are contiguous to the Camino Real, the different passages, the routes adjacent to the cliffs, and the existing ravines, in order to have the appropriate information, and with particular attention to the Channel of Santa Barbara which stretches along the coast and Sierra of La Cienegüilla some 24 to 26 leagues [63 to 68 miles], with a width of half a league [1.35 miles] where it begins.

The road lies partly on the beach at the foot of high bluffs, providing a narrow passageway between them and the seashore. This makes it necessary to travel partly in the water even at low tide, and partly across ridges and frequent deep and narrow arroyos. There are few level areas between these arroyos, which together with the considerable number of natives, probably no less than 8 to 10 thousand living in 21 major *rancherías* found in the nearby mountains and close to the beach near which the road is located, so rugged in parts during the rainy season that passage of an arroyo is made with difficulty, requiring great skill in managing the horses. All of which emphasizes not only the obvious risk to which small parties traversing this road of necessity are exposed, but also that if some incident antagonizes these natives, the route will be blocked. Therefore,

---

[1]Tibesar, *Writings of Serra*, III, 115.

until we settle this Channel with soldiers competent to control diplomatically those Indians, we cannot count on free communications between these settlements, and any unfortunate incident in it [the Channel area] will cause us trouble.

Passing from these thoughts, I turned to a study of which sites would be suitable for occupation along the Channel and the number of troops needed to garrison them. I find it necessary to have the two settlements of missions already proposed, one next to the arroyo and *ranchería* of La Asunta at the entrance of the Channel coming from San Diego, and the other next to the *ranchería* of Point Concepción, commonly called La Espada, given the name of La Purísima Concepción.[2] But even after these settlements are garrisoned, I believe that with the slow pace of the spiritual conversion, even if the contiguous *rancherías* at both ends [of the Channel] are converted, there will always be the threat that communications will be severed whenever the *rancherías* of the center, which are the most numerous and united, decide to oppose us, which our presence must be presumed to impart motives. Therefore I consider the occupation of the center necessary, establishing in it a fort and a third mission, this one with the name Santa Barbara if Your Excellency is kind enough to give its establishment your approval.

The troops which normally should garrison these posts (considering the arrogance, vivacity, vigor and fondness for swords which is observed in these natives and distinguishes them from all the others of this California) are a sergeant and fourteen privates at each one of the first two missions, and in the fort, one lieutenant, one sergeant, two corporals and twenty six soldiers. These garrisons guarantee control of the *rancherías* near the three settlements, or part of them, and the assurance of peace and security from the remaining. They will be able to be kept in check, although I consider it necessary always to maintain the existence of the fort and under its protection, the mission. After a time [the mission] can be located apart if it is advantageous in order to increase production from the land and its waters.

---

[2]*Espada* (sword) is the name of the original rancho that extended from Jalama Beach to Point Pedernales. It received its name from an incident that occurred on August 27, 1769, when the Portolá expedition was approaching Point Concepción. An Indian of a nearby village stole the sword of one of the soldiers. Another Indian ran after the thief and returned the sword to its owner. The soldiers called the village the *ranchería* of Espada.

The site which I observed to be most suitable for establishment of the fort is in the vicinity of Mescaltitán [the Goleta airport area], the three towns opposite Yslado [the hill upon which the Goleta Sanitary District plant is located] and in a dominant and open place [possibly the site of the campus of the University of California, Santa Barbara]. But having to consider the problem of defense and the availability of cultivatable fields, a special reconnaissance is necessary in order to find out more about it...Soldiers must come equipped with weapons and mounted, with two cannon of 4 [meaning two cannon using four pound cannon balls] for the presidio if Your Excellency approves its founding.

In this case, the shipment of clothing and provisions must be sent by ship, and for this there will have to be a determination as to which of the bays or harbors of the Channel will be more secure to anchor the ships and unload their cargo. Without doubt it should be near the site marked for the fort, concerning which Frigate Lieutenant Diego Choquet, who anchored in the year 1776 next to the three villages of the Channel, will be able to advise you.[3]

Mail delivery was slow and uncertain and the wheels of government ground even slower than today's. Therefore the elapsed time between Neve's decision to establish a settlement along the Santa Barbara Channel and its accomplishment was lengthy. Fr. Junípero Serra was the principal complainant. In a letter to the new Father Guardian of San Fernando College dated August 19, 1778, Serra wrote:

It is my fault — I do not know whether it be formal or material — that San Buenaventura has not been founded now for many years. It was started, and it even appeared in print from the start that the place assigned to the said mission was at the entrance of the Santa Barbara Channel, near the settlement called La Asumpta [*sic*]. Because a larger number of escort soldiers was needed in that locality than in the other missions, I could never manage to have the foundation started. And so San Buenaventura is still waiting, after

---

[3]According to Thurman, *Department of San Blas*, p. 198, Lt. Diego Choquet was aboard the ship *El Príncipe*. According to a letter dated October 8, 1776, in Tibesar, *Writings of Serra*, III, 73, Serra traveled on this ship, leaving Monterey June 29th and arriving at San Diego July 11th. Apparently the ship anchored at Goleta on this voyage. Choquet's description of this voyage has not, so far, been discovered by this author.

eight have already been established; and it was to have been the third.[4]

Approval for founding of the presidio, and with it Santa Barbara and San Buenaventura missions, was finally given in a letter dated September 3, 1778, to Governor Neve in Monterey from Teodoro de Croix, Commanding General of the Interior Provinces of New Spain from 1776 to 1783. From the general's headquarters at Arizpe, Sonora, official approval was given for "erection of a presidio with a garrison composed of a lieutenant, a sergeant, two corporals and twenty-six soldiers (exclusive of the mission guards) in the center of the Channel of Santa Barbara, and, under the protection of the presidio, a mission with the same name and another named San Buenaventura."[5] The elapsed time between the date of Governor Neve's recommendation and the Commanding General's approval was 457 days! The same letter also approved establishment of the two pueblos of Los Angeles and San Jose. However, the pueblo of San Jose had been provisionally founded and settled by Neve on November 29, 1776.

Acknowledgement of Croix's letter by Neve was dated April 3, 1779. In it he states that he is informed that establishment of the presidio and missions on the Channel of Santa Barbara has been approved; that once the Channel is garrisoned, the garrisons of the other presidios should be reduced; and that the burden on the Royal Treasury will be reduced to 6,213 *pesos*, 4 *tomines* and 9⅕ *granos*.[6]

Father Serra's dream of having a mission named San Buena-

---

[4]Tibesar, *Writings of Serra*, III, 243.

[5]The Archives of California, as recorded by Bancroft in transcript form, are organized into various subsections, such as Provincial Records, Provincial State Papers, etc. These will be cited in the footnotes simply by giving the subsection, the volume number and the pages. Provincial State Papers, II, 293-94.

[6]Junípero Serra Collection 781, April 3, 1779. A gold *tomín* was one eighth of a *peso*. A silver *real* was one eighth of a *peso*. A *grano*, gold or silver, was one twelfth of a *tomín* or a *real* or one 96th of a *peso*.

ventura was finally to be realized, but always the planner, he had mixed feelings as expressed in a letter dated March 29, 1779.

> The news that came by the last mail under other conditions would have made me dance with joy. But, now, conditions being what they are, I can foresee what lies ahead, and what it gives me is an increase in my worries. The news is this: as soon as possible, a presidio and three missions are to be founded in the Santa Barbara Channel, and when these couriers get to Loreto, Don Fernando [de Rivera y Moncada, Lieutenant Governor of Baja California] has to take ship for the opposite coast [the mainland across the Gulf of California] to gather together troops and animals.
>
> The three missions are San Buenaventura on the site chosen; La Purísima Concepción near the Point of that name; and Mission Santa Barbara in the middle, near the presidio, the name of which we do not know. I have already put before them some difficulties, and what they say in reply gives me little satisfaction. Therefore if I cannot do so now, I hope to put them before our College [of San Fernando] when the boat sails back in order that they may make definite arrangements there before sending religious [priests]. But in the midst of all my troubles I am happy because children are born amidst pain.[7]

At least one of Father Serra's troubles was explained in a letter to Fr. Juan Figuer of Mission San Diego, written the next day. During a discussion concerning establishment of the Santa Barbara Presidio, Serra had told Neve that his greatest anxiety was about the religious that would be assigned to the mission of the Saint in that vicinity.

> The annoyances, the insulting and scandalous conduct of the soldiers, I took for granted, would immediately be the same as we had experienced in other places which were connected with presidios. Perhaps this one would be worse.[8]

Serra, whose whole life was devoted to converting the

---

[7]Tibesar, *Writings of Serra*, III, 297, 299.
[8]Tibesar, *Writings of Serra*, III, 305.

Indians and reducing immorality among them, felt constantly frustrated by the behavior of the soldiers in taking advantage of the Indian girls, and he blamed the Governor for this situation by not punishing the culprits. Yet he knew the soldiers were necessary to guard the missionaries against any hostile acts.

The same day, Serra wrote to Croix thanking him for his decision and stating that he, Serra, had passed through all the *rancherías* of the Channel for the fourth time the previous November and the inhabitants "as always were charming and attractive, waiting silently for the Holy Gospel... I ask Your Lordship, with all due deference, to take such measures as seem adequate to eradicate bad example and provocations to revolt which, among so large a population, would necessarily produce deplorable results."[9]

Shortly after his arrival in Alta California, Governor Neve commenced improving its defenses, which up until 1777 consisted of the three presidios of San Diego, Monterey and San Francisco. All were merely a collection of huts within palisade-type defensive walls, totally inadequate for protection against attack.[10] By July 1778 he had had the defense wall at Monterey rebuilt with stone eleven feet high and four feet thick and some of the interior buildings were completed. At San Francisco, the defense wall was built of adobe, soon undermined and destroyed by the rains of early 1779. At San Diego, stones were being collected for foundations.[11]

There now ensued voluminous correspondence between the Commanding General, the Viceroy, the Governor and various other officials setting the stage for recruiting soldiers for Santa Barbara and settlers for Los Angeles; for purchasing horses, mules and cattle; outfitting the soldiers and set-

[9]Tibesar, *Writings of Serra*, III, 311, 313.
[10]Bancroft, *California*, I, 331.
[11]Provincial Record, I, 90-91.

tlers with clothing, armament and supplies; arranging transportation; and providing funds.[12]

In detailed instructions given by General Croix to Captain
Fernando de Rivera y Moncada, Lieutenant Governor of
Baja California, dated December 27, 1779, Rivera was
ordered to recruit soldiers for the Santa Barbara Presidio and
settlers for the pueblos of Los Angeles and San Jose. Soldiers
for the presidio and Channel missions were to be recruited in
Sinaloa and Sonora. They had to be married men, healthy,
strong, able to endure hardship and of good character to set
an example for the natives. They were committed to ten years
of service, but all had to be volunteers, and no exaggeration as
to opportunities was permitted by recruiters. Because there
were many bachelor soldiers already in California, unmarried
female relatives of the settlers were encouraged to accompany
the cavalcade.[13]

A total of twenty-five experienced soldiers, including
three sergeants and two corporals, to be replaced by recruits,
were transferred from the presidial companies of Sonora to
the California presidios. The total recruit requirement in
California for settling the two pueblos and manning the
Santa Barbara Presidio was set at twenty-four families and

---

[12]Copies of many of these letters and reports were obtained by Father Francis Guest, O.F.M., from the *Archivo General de la Nación* in Mexico City in 1964 and are on file at the Santa Barbara Mission Archive-Library, where he is archivist. Few have been translated. Two documents for which this author searched for a considerable length of time because of their particular interest to this study were finally found in the Bancroft Library microfilm collection. They are the *memorias* or orders for clothing, food and supplies expected to be needed by the garrison at the Santa Barbara Presidio, dated July 19, 1779 and signed by Governor Neve three years before the presidio was founded. These were found in Mexico City in the *Archivo General de la Nación, Provincias Internas, tomo* 121. The same microfilms and the documents obtained by Fr. Guest from Mexico City also revealed many other *memorias* and *facturas* or bills of lading itemizing the contents of shipments from the San Blas supply depot to the California presidios and missions during the years 1775 to 1812. These have been used by Dr. Norman Neuerburg to document the furnishings of the presidio chapels and some of the mission churches.

[13]Marion Parks (trans.), "Instructions for the Recruital of Soldiers and Settlers for California—Expedition of 1781," pp. 189-203. The original document is found in *A.G.N., Provincias Internas, tomo* 122.

fifty-nine men, but since twenty-five recruits were to replace those taken from the frontier presidios, only thirty-four were to go to California. The rendezvous point was San Miguel de Horcasitas in Sonora, north of Hermosillo. From there they were to travel to Alamos, southeast of Guaymas, for equipment, clothing, provisions and livestock.

Commencing with the day on which they enlisted, each recruit was to receive two *reales* in cash (about 0.25 *pesos*) per day or its equivalent in provisions for use when traveling through unpopulated areas or on the frontier, reserving the rest of his pay to cover the costs of the march and equipment. Provision was made for recruiting at Guadalajara in case the full complement was not completed at Alamos, that group traveling by ship from San Blas.

From Alamos, forty-two soldiers, of whom thirty had their families, commenced the trek in April of 1781 by way of Tucson and the Colorado River to San Gabriel Mission near Los Angeles. They were accompanied as far as the Colorado River by a contingent of soldiers from the Sonora presidios. Those not in the entourage went by ship from San Blas or from Guaymas to the Presidio of Loreto in Baja California.[14]

This entire operation was no mean accomplishment. Rivera was directed to recruit a total of twenty-four families to settle Los Angeles and add to those at San Jose and fifty-nine soldiers for the presidios and mission *escoltas* (guards). In addition to all the equipment and supplies, he had to purchase a total of 551 mules, 256 horses, 60 brood mares, 80 burros, 6 donkeys, 4 stallions and 4 geldings, a total of 961 animals of which 153 mules and 102 horses were designated for the Presidio of Santa Barbara. In a letter dated February 10, 1780, Governor Neve received a copy of Croix's instructions to Rivera which set forth the bureaucratic red tape necessary to account for all the expenditures. It also ordered

---

[14]Bancroft, *California*, I, 340-45.

founding of the presidio and three missions along the Santa
Barbara Channel in addition to the two pueblos. The part
requesting assistance from the Viceroy reads as follows:

> Third: As the aforementioned provisions and goods are to be
> sent through the Port of San Blas, it will be suitable that a recon-
> naissance of the Channel, like that which Frigate Lieutenant Don
> Diego Choquet made, will be repeated ahead of time, so that the
> unloading of the provisions be done there, and if that is not possi-
> ble, at the Port of San Diego.
>
> Fourth: For the construction of the new presidio, there is needed
> 4,000 *pesos* in goods which with the tax of 150 percent will reduce
> the cost of construction to 1,200 *pesos* (so to speak), the forwarding
> of which to San Blas is urgent, so that the Governor of the Califor-
> nias may arrange its disposition.
>
> Fifth: The Governor has asked for two cannons *de a 4* [using
> four-pound cannon balls] and suitable cartridges, half of them
> grapeshot, for the defense of the aforementioned presidio and that
> the transporting be done by way of San Blas.
>
> Sixth: The three missions which are to be established in the
> Channel for the glory of the Purísima Concepción, Santa Barbara
> and San Buenaventura, need six friars from the Apostolic College
> of San Fernando [in Mexico City] and their departure from Mex-
> ico should be prompt, sending four through the Port of San Blas
> and the other two to this Province of Sonora, so that they may
> arrive here by July or August of this year.
>
> Seventh: In order to establish the Mission of San Buenaventura,
> 1,000 *pesos* are granted, but we need equal aid for each one of the
> other two in the Channel. As to the additional two thousand *pesos*,
> we can obtain them in Mexico from the alms of the Apostolic Col-
> lege of San Fernando, and expend them for the vestments, sacred
> vessels and good of the church.
>
> Eighth: The Governor deems it advisable that in each one of the
> three new missions they support six day-laborers with salary and
> rations for a term of three years.[15]

In October 1780, Governor Neve requested that the
Viceroy arrange that goods, merchandise, foodstuffs, cannon

---

[15]Provincial State Papers, II, 376-86.

and munitions he had requisitioned to supply the troops at the presidio and missions of the Santa Barbara Channel be sent in the supply ship sailing to Monterey, and be unloaded at the Channel "if the troops are present at that time."[16] This was accomplished, as will be seen later, in August of 1782.

More orders to Rivera concerning the expedition were transmitted by letter dated December 18, 1780, from Croix to Governor Neve. He wrote:

> Your Excellency should also arrange for receipt of the field tents, pack train equipment, sacks, leather chests and the rest of the goods which the Royal Exchequer has paid for, distributing what can be used by the presidial companies, and corresponding charges will be made to the gratuity funds and the surplus goods will be deposited in some one of the royal warehouses, where they will be cared for and stored. It seems to me that when there is an opportunity, the field tents should be returned to Alamos in case later there might be other pack trains of families.[17]

The Commanding General was sympathetic to the hardships and dangers of the 950-mile trip by land from Alamos to San Gabriel. He commanded:

> Take particular care that the officers and families who are to be transported by ship travel with the greatest possible comforts and that they have plenty of provisions. Also, arrange the march by land with equal concern that there is no lack of provisions and that the day's march be reasonable so that the women and children do not tire, and so that the horses be kept in good condition without straying or being lost. Lastly, see that the troops carry out their duties perfectly, staying together on marches and executing your orders with vigilance and zeal in order to prevent assaults by hostile Indians, and in order not to offend in the least way the friendly and peaceful nations living between the Colorado River and New California.[18]

An interesting observation appears in a letter dated Janu-

---

[16]Provincial Record, II, 248.
[17]Provincial State Papers, II, 405-06.
[18]Provincial State Papers, II, pp. 409-10.

ary 20, 1781, from Neve to Commanding General Croix. Neve acknowledges an order giving to him the final say as to where the pueblos of San Jose and Los Angeles are to be located. He also comments that he is aware that Croix is trying to place the new Channel presidio on land suitable for crops so that, in time, there can be another settlement under the shelter and in the vicinity of the presidio, but that this is not possible because of the great scarcity of water in the areas bordering the Santa Barbara Channel. He states that he investigated the places indicated between San Diego and the Channel, and although in several he found abundant land and water, he saw the impracticality of utilizing the water unless conduits of rough stone and mortar were constructed, a project not feasible at that time. He states that he considers the Porciúncula (Los Angeles) River as the only dependable and practicable source although it is a distance of thirty leagues from the Santa Barbara Presidio site.[19] Obviously Neve could not foresee such engineering feats as the Cachuma Dam Project, the Central Valley Project or bringing Colorado River water to Los Angeles.

The land expedition, together with its escort from Sonora, arrived at San Gabriel by way of Tucson on July 14, 1781. Some of the men who accompanied Anza on his historic expedition to San Francisco in 1776 served as guides. The balance of the settlers and soldier-recruits crossed the Gulf of California from Guaymas to San Luis Bay (apparently what is now known as Bahía San Luis Gonzaga), from whence they followed the route of the Portolá expedition north to San Diego and San Gabriel. On August 18, 1781, this group arrived at San Gabriel where they were immediately quarantined, some of the children having just recovered from smallpox.[20]

---

[19]Provincial Record, II, 257.
[20]Bancroft, *California*, I, 340-45.

The combined group camped at San Gabriel during the winter of 1781-1782. Neve decided that the settlements of San Jose and the Channel area had to be delayed until spring because of the difficulty of transporting supplies and constructing shelters during the rainy season. There was still enough time during good weather to found Los Angeles at its nearby site, and on September 4, 1781, the pueblo was founded with twelve settlers and their families, forty-six persons in all. Rivera had been unable to recruit the planned-for twenty-four families.

In the meantime an event occurred that may have played a part in delaying the founding of Mission Santa Barbara concurrently with the founding of the presidio as had taken place at San Diego, Monterey and San Francisco. At Santa Barbara, the mission was not founded until four years after the founding of the presidio.

During 1780 and 1781, two pueblos with missions, La Purísima Concepción and San Pedro and San Pablo de Bicuñer, had been established in the vicinity of what is now Yuma on the Colorado River. On July 17, 1781, the Indians attacked these settlements and massacred the inhabitants. At least forty-six people were killed, including Captain Rivera, who had just led the settlers and recruits from Alamos to the Colorado River and, having seen them safely on their way to San Gabriel under an adequate escort, had returned to the east bank of the Colorado to recuperate his horses and cattle for the rest of the trip.[21]

Measures to subdue the Indians and counteract the damage done by them occupied Governor Neve's forces for some time. Neve's previous decision to delay the foundations along the Santa Barbara Channel was therefore fortunate. His later decision to found the presidio but not the mission at Santa Barbara may have stemmed from his desire to establish mili-

[21]Bancroft, *California*, I, 362-67; Chapman, *A History of California*, pp. 330-42.

tary protection before the missionaries began their work because of the catastrophe on the Colorado River. On October 29, 1781, Neve wrote the Viceroy that establishment of the presidio of the Channel had not been realized because of the lack of training and the exhausted state of the recruits who had arrived, the fatigue of the horses and the disaster on the Colorado. The founding, he explained, would occur after the rainy season.[22]

At San Gabriel, the Santa Barbara company for the presidio was being formed, organized and trained under Lt. José Francisco Ortega, who had been commander of the garrison at the San Diego Presidio since 1774 and who in September had been appointed commander of the Santa Barbara company by the Governor. Forty small palisade huts with flat roofs had been built there to shelter the soldiers and their families. Seven privates and a corporal were withdrawn from each of the companies of the Monterey and San Diego presidios as a cadre to train the recruits.[23]

By February of 1782, Neve decided that hostilities on the Colorado River had quieted down to the point where it was safe to proceed with the Channel establishments. He wrote Fr. Serra asking for two missionaries, one for Mission San Buenaventura and one for Mission Santa Barbara. The former mission had highest priority for Serra, who had arranged to have money and furnishings set aside for it as early as 1769. Serra, therefore, traveled from Monterey to San Gabriel to participate in the founding, arriving March 19, 1782. At a meeting with the Governor that day, they decided to found San Buenaventura Mission at the southerly end of the Santa Barbara Channel, then proceed with the founding of the presidio and mission of Santa Barbara at a midway

---

[22]Provincial Record, II, 308.

[23]Provincial State Papers, III, 302; Provincial State Papers, Presidios I, 2-3; and Provincial Record, II, 306.

point along the Channel.[24] Thus the preparations for settle-
ment of that stretch of California coastline bordering on the
Santa Barbara Channel, including the founding of the Santa
Barbara Presidio and Missions San Buenaventura, Santa
Barbara and, later, La Purísima Concepción, were com-
pleted.

---

[24]Geiger (trans.), *Palóu's Life of Serra*, p. 220.

Chapter Four

The Expedition to Santa Barbara

According to his service record, the commanding officer-designate of the new Santa Barbara Presidio, Lt. José Francisco Ortega, was born in 1734 in Celaya in the Province of Guanajuato. Located about 120 miles northwest of Mexico City, it has a present population of about 80,000. At age nineteen, he was in Loreto, Baja California, where he married the twelve-year-old daughter of Juan Carrillo of the garrison of the local presidio. He enlisted in 1755, and was promoted to corporal in ten months, to sergeant five months later, and to lieutenant in August 1773.[1]

When Father Serra recommended Ortega as a replacement for Military Commander Pedro Fages, Ortega was still a sergeant, but he had been promised a promotion when he was advance guard with the Portolá expedition and was the first European to see San Francisco Bay. Serra describes Ortega as being firm without rigidity, and having prudence and common sense.[2] In Celaya, he had gained brief experience in management as manager of a storehouse and shop. Serra said he was conscientious, alert, honorable and capable, and, concerning his rank, that Fages was only a lieutenant when he was appointed to his position of command. Ortega's service record, signed by Fages, gave him a good character reference. Ortega was a *soldado de cuera* like most of the other soldiers of the California frontier, whereas Fages was a mem-

[1]Luann Powell, Genealogical Chart of José Francisco Ortega, MS.
[2]Tibesar, *Writings of Serra*, I, 301-07.

ber of the elitist Catalan Volunteers. Serra considered that this gave Ortega an advantage in dealing with the daily problems of the other soldiers.

Ortega had been involved in the plans for the Santa Barbara settlements before he was appointed commanding officer of the Santa Barbara garrison. On April 22, 1780, Governor Neve informed Croix that he had ordered Ortega to make an inspection of the entire Channel area to find potential sites for the presidio and missions. Ortega reported back that he had found the ideal site, plenty of water that could be diverted for irrigation, and fertile land with stone and timber available, although there was a shortage of pasturage.[3] Apparently this was the future site of the San Buenaventura Mission. Neve was so impressed by the report that he wondered if perhaps the new pueblo of Los Angeles might be established there.

Neve himself inspected the various sites in May 1781. He discovered that timber was in short supply at Santa Barbara, meaning that construction of the roofs of buildings would have to be delayed until beams could be obtained. The only timber nearby that was suitable for construction was on La Cumbre Peak back of Santa Barbara. At a greater distance, it could be found at both a site near Figueroa Mountain in the Santa Ynez Valley and across the Channel on Santa Cruz Island. There were plenty of oaks along the arroyos and in Montecito, but these were not tall enough to produce long beams. Cutting and importing beams from Monterey depended on the annual arrival of the supply ships from San Blas. Furthermore, adobe blocks could be made efficiently only in warm weather. These factors undoubtedly influenced his decision to postpone the founding of the Santa Barbara Presidio from the winter of 1781 to the spring of 1782.

---

[3]Beilharz, *Neve*, p. 113.

Ortega was to be in command of the presidio at its head-quarters in Santa Barbara, but the *escoltas* (guard escorts) were to be stationed at a considerable distance from the presidio, at San Buenaventura and at La Purísima. Neve therefore drafted a set of instructions applicable to Ortega and to the sergeants in command of the *escoltas*. Dated March 6, 1782, about three weeks before the expedition left Mission San Gabriel, the instructions gave top priority to bringing in to the presidio, one after another, the chiefs of the Indian villages to inform them that "we intend to settle there by order of our very powerful King, who loves them and wants to have them under his sovereign protection, to defend them from their enemies, and that they be taught to know God and His sacred law by which they may be saved."[4]

After completion of the ceremonies founding the San Buenaventura Mission and the presidio, top priority was to be given to protection of the troops and their families from possible Indian attack. A stockade of earth had to be erected. It was to be located so that it would not interfere with the building of the walls and bastions that had to be constructed later so that the presidio would be enclosed. In the center, structures with roofs of branches or reeds were to be built for the comfort and protection of the troops and their families, but they should not be built until the stockade was finished. Next, in order, came construction of a large storeroom, the chapel, the guardhouse, the officers' quarters, temporary quarters for the padres, and those necessary for the families. The same procedures, including a stockade, were to be followed at the missions.

The troops and the servants were responsible for all the construction, since the result was for the comfort and protection of all. At San Buenaventura, a granary and warehouses

---

[4]Provincial State Papers, III, 36; Bancroft, *California*, I, 372-75.

were to be constructed in which to store reserve supplies for the presidio and the rest of the missions. Perhaps this provision was included partly because Neve realized that the land surrounding San Buenaventura settlement was far more fertile than that at Santa Barbara and could produce more food.

During and after the construction period, the Indians were to be discouraged from gathering at the site, without showing any distrust of them. They were to leave their bows and arrows outside the enclosure, stay away from the dwellings, and go home at night. The troops were to keep in mind that the Indians outnumbered them and that this might give the Indians ideas of what they could do.

Detailed instructions were included for day and night security against surprise attack. Soldiers were prohibited from entering an Indian village except when escorting a priest. Any soldier who violated this order was to suffer "fifteen days detention in the guardhouse doing guard duty the first quarter of the night or on the dawn patrol, plus four lashes, even though no complaint or scandal resulted from the act." Initially, soldiers could not have cattle with them at the presidio, except the six or eight calves that officers were allowed to have. From time to time, cattle could be rounded up for butchering. This way the Indians would not be so tempted to steal cattle.

Punishments for Indian misdeeds were spelled out. If an Indian wounded a horse or mule with a bow and arrow, he was to be given twelve to fifteen lashes, warned not to do it again, and then released. If the death of the horse or mule resulted, the culprit would receive twenty-five lashes and be kept in the stocks fifteen days. To release him, the chief of his village would have to appear and the crime be described to him. It would be explained that the crime warranted much greater punishment but, since he was loved by the Spaniards, he would be forgiven if he gave assurance that he would not do it again. Such punishments may seem severe, but actually they were lenient compared to penalties imposed on Spanish soldiers for similar offenses.

Damaged swords or lances were to be sold to the settlers, not discarded, because the Indians valued highly any piece of steel and could fashion weapons from it. A mail service was established, with precautions against the courier loitering at his destination and with explicit requirements for recording the day, month and hour of delivery at each establishment.

Recognition was given to the problem of supplying the Channel installations with corn, beans and other grains which had to be carried on muleback from San Gabriel Mission. Cargos were to be delivered to San Buenaventura for storage because, up to that site, "in all seasons the mule trains can operate." This provides another reason why Neve ordered sufficient storage space at San Buenaventura to provide for the presidio at Santa Barbara.

The instructions then continued with a procedure that would be strongly opposed by the president of the missions, Father Junípero Serra. Neve had already tipped his hand to Serra by asking him to send two missionaries to the Channel, one for San Buenaventura and one for Santa Barbara Mission. In Title Fifteen of his 1781 *Reglamento*, Neve had specified that the three Channel missions would each have two priests at the start, but that after their founding, each new mission would have only one priest.[5] Now he was reneging and providing for only one at each of the Channel missions. Serra considered this a dangerous proposal, unfair to the priests and damaging to the program for converting the pagans.

Neve's order to Ortega contained one other program that was anathema to Serra, namely an administrative arrange-

---

[5]Johnson (trans.), *Regulations for Governing*, p. 51.

ment that had been tried as an experiment at the Colorado River. Serra attributed the massacre at the river to the failure of this experiment, the setting up of a sort of conglomerate pueblo, mission and presidio.[6] The Indians would be left in their villages and not be brought in to the mission. Their conversion, education and training would take place at their home village. Serra believed that they would be subject to the temptations of their pagan way of life and to the ridicule and exhortations of the Indians who opposed conversion.

Neve gave as his reason for the change that:

> these missions, necessarily, have to differ in their plan and arrangement from the others...as dictated by the location of the villages, the limited width of the [level] land, the distribution of natives, their movement, plentiful food supplies that nourish them such as fish, game, grains, and other products of the soil that they trade with the mountain people whose conduct and direction are not yet under our Catholic religion. They should not be hindered nor obliged to adjust to a new settlement, work or otherwise be separated from their villages. To attempt it would be to transform them from friends to implacable enemies.
>
> In addition, excluding the Mission of San Buenaventura, the land of the two remaining settlements does not permit establishment of a dependable grain field; consequently they will never be able to feed the growing numbers of Christians they are bound to have. They can barely succeed in feeding some boys and adults that are taking instruction for a few days. This is assuming that the King so desires it, namely the advantage and undeniable soundness of leaving them in their unfettered native freedom. It is essential that these natives rule themselves in everything as provided by the laws of the Kingdom, and that we, for our part, watch continually to aid the Reverend Minister in the important primary objective of conversion, contributing to it with our example and way of life. Let this be the means to guide them in our friendship and to attract them, so that they become interested in communicating with us and the exchanges they make of their goods for ours, and to wish to imitate

---

[6]Tibesar, *Writings of Serra*, IV, 103.

us in hard work at which they are so apt because of their sharpness and intelligence as demonstrated by the admirable construction of their canoes.[7]

Several items in Neve's instructions deserve comment. First, as a good soldier, he warned against the possibility that the Indians would turn hostile, and demanded precautions against a surprise attack. Second, in the same vein, he ordered that the initial structures be located so as not to interfere with the permanent (adobe) construction. Naturally, if the permanent buildings were built outside of and surrounding the temporary construction, the trenches or ditches and the embankments would protect the garrison until the permanent defensive walls were completed. For this reason, when land acquisition and demolition of modern buildings at the Santa Barbara site reaches the stage where archaeology can be undertaken in the central portion of the quadrangle, it is possible that trenches and post holes of the original palisade structures may be uncovered within the parade ground area. Third, Neve stressed that the three Channel missions must differ in their operation from the eight already founded. He believed that the Indians should be allowed to remain in their villages, and go to the missions only for instruction and religious activities. The missions would raise only enough crops to provide for the missionaries. Neve, of course, was counting on the pueblos (Los Angeles and San Jose) to raise sufficient food to provision the presidios.

This concept was completely contrary to the program of the missionaries. They were convinced that only by housing the Indians at the mission where they would be under Franciscan supervision twenty-four hours a day could they, by their example, convert and change the life-style of the Indians. They had to teach them the Spanish language; loyalty to

---

[7]Provincial State Papers, III, 39-41.

the King; the habits of sanitation, work and cooperation with others; obedience and respect that exemplified the character of civilized persons; and the precepts of the Christian religion. If allowed to remain in their villages, they would constantly be under the influence of pagan Indians and exposed to the evils of their aboriginal customs.

When Serra received word that the founding of San Buenaventura was imminent, he sent word to San Diego asking that Father Pedro Cambón, who had just returned from the Philippines as chaplain on the frigate *Princesa*, meet him at San Gabriel. At their meeting with Neve on March 19th, it was decided that Cambón would remain at San Buenaventura as soon as it was founded and that Father Serra would temporarily serve at the Santa Barbara Mission until the arrival of the expected six missionaries being sent by the College of San Fernando in Mexico City.[8] No mention was made in the record of who would serve at La Purísima Mission, but since there was no priest available, it must be assumed that plans for its founding at that time had, at least temporarily, been abandoned.

On March 26, 1782, the expedition departed from San Gabriel. There were some 200 people and about 200 horses and mules in the procession, "more people than had ever before been seen gathered together in these missions," according to Palóu.[9] There were sixty soldiers including the commander of the new presidio, an ensign, three sergeants, and two corporals. The Governor went along, with ten soldiers of the company belonging to Monterey. There were the muleteers with the trains of utensils and food supplies, some servants and some Indian neophytes to aid in establishment of the mission. In addition, there were the wives and children of the soldiers. Based upon a census taken in 1784, the fami-

---

[8]Geiger, *Palóu's Life of Serra*, pp. 219-20.
[9]Geiger, *Palóu's Life of Serra*, pp. 220-21.

lies of the soldiers totaled more than one hundred women and children.

The column probably extended about a mile from point to rear guard, all under the leadership of Governor Neve. About midnight of the first day's journey, however, a courier from San Gabriel caught up with the column, bringing the Governor a message from Lt. Fages. Fages had been sent by General Croix to investigate the massacre at the Colorado River the previous July. Croix gave Neve the choice of proceeding with the founding of the Channel settlements or mounting a campaign against the Yuma Indians. Neve chose to proceed with the Channel establishments, but returned to San Gabriel to confer with Fages, giving orders to Ortega to proceed to San Buenaventura. In case of delay, Ortega was to proceed with the founding of San Buenaventura Mission and wait there for him.

The expedition arrived at the present site of San Buenaventura Mission on Good Friday of Holy Week, March 29, 1782. The following day a large cross was erected and a rough shelter to serve as a temporary chapel was built. On Easter Sunday, March 31st, Father Serra sang the first Mass there, the soldiers took formal possession of the site and the mission was founded. In describing the founding in a letter dated March 31st to Father Lasuén, Serra wrote: "But now, on account of what has taken place on the Colorado River, the other foundations will be delayed, and all the people here, together with their provisions, etc., will stay where they are, unless something new intervenes."[10] Governor Neve rejoined the expedition on or about April 9th.

Immediately after the founding ceremonies, the soldiers, with the help of the Indians from the adjacent village of *Shisholop*, began constructing the palisade-type mission. Under the direction of Father Cambón, they began diverting

[10]Tibesar, *Writings of Serra*, IV, 103.

water from the Ventura River through an aqueduct to the mission site. When Neve rejoined the group, work was well along, and he could see that the design repeated the old plan of the earlier missions which provided for Indians to live at the mission. According to Palóu:

> he did not say a word, despite the fact that he had planned and recommended, as was later learned, that these missions should be founded after the new method followed along the Colorado River. It may be that the change in success and outcome, of which he heard from Señor Fages, was the thing that opened his eyes and caused him to change both his ideas and intentions.[11]

There are other explanations for Neve's failure to react to their disregard of his instructions. Beilharz believes that Neve did not want to tip his hand yet as to the plans he had for the other two Channel missions, and wanted to put off the confrontation with Serra as long as he could, so that Serra suspected nothing.[12] Engelhardt surmises that Neve thought it politic to postpone his plan until Santa Barbara was reached.[13] Bancroft suggests that possibly the nature of the instructions was not available to Ortega when he arrived at Ventura.[14]

This latter seems to be the most probable explanation because the manuscript in the Bancroft Library is dated October 1, 1782, and is labeled "Pedro Fages to Lieutenant-Commander José de Ortega, transmitted from Felipe de Neve." It is quite possible that when the expedition reached San Buenaventura, Ortega had not seen the instructions. Otherwise, why is there no record that Neve, Ortega's immediate military superior, did not punish or reprimand him for disobedience, a serious crime in the military?

In Neve's *Reglamento* of 1781, he ordered that there would

---

[11]Geiger, *Palóu's Life of Serra*, p. 229.
[12]Beilharz, *Neve*, p. 120.
[13]Engelhardt, *San Buenaventura*, p. 17.
[14]Bancroft, *California*, I, 376.

be only one priest at each mission and he made no provision for supplying a mission with farming tools and instructors in agriculture. The farm implements and other equipment to establish San Buenaventura Mission on the basis that the Indians would live and work at the mission had been stored at San Gabriel since 1771. They were brought along when the expedition left that mission to found San Buenaventura. The problem created by Neve's failure to order tools therefore took care of itself. For a time, at least, Father Cambón could manage as the only priest at the mission.[15]

There was no love lost between Father Serra and Governor Neve. It must be remembered that Neve had been ordered to arrest the Jesuits in the Zacatecas area and, later, to administer their property. Possibly he placed the Franciscan, Fr. Serra, in a similar category as the Jesuits and therefore an adversary of the King. Neve had actively opposed Serra's power of confirmation which had been approved by the Pope, the King and the Viceroy in 1776.[16]

In 1778 while Serra was confirming mare than two thousand converts, Neve questioned his right to confirm on the basis that a secular royal council may not have sanctioned that right, as was required by law. When Neve asked Serra to prove that he had the right by showing him the documents, Serra said he did not have the documents, having sent them to the Father Guardian at the College of San Fernando in Mexico. Neve did not believe Serra, and through channels, he then secured an order preventing Serra from exercising the right.[17]

In a letter to General Croix, Neve wrote concerning Serra:

---

[15]Beilharz, *Neve*, pp. 119-20.

[16]Bancroft, *California*, I, 326.

[17]Confirmation is the sacrament performed by a bishop on a person who has been baptized but has not received religious instruction. Godparents vow that their godchild will accept the Christian faith. After the child has grown and has received instruction, his faith is confirmed.

There is no mischief these religious will not attempt if exasperated, such is their boundless unbelievable pride. My politeness and moderation over more than four years have not been enough to turn them from the hostility with which they engage in surreptitious conspiracies against the government and its laws. There is no means whatsoever they would scorn. He [Serra] knows how to feign compliance in matters put before him, as well as how to avoid it, just as he is doing in this case.[18]

Serra's one fear, as expressed in a letter to the Guardian of the College of San Fernando, was that people would say that the Governor had more power regarding religious matters than the religious (which in many respects he did) and that they might conclude that previous confirmation actions were improper. Serra did cease administering the rite, but won out in the end when, on May 19, 1781, the Governor wrote him that approvals by higher authority had been cleared and that Serra could continue with the confirmations.[19]

Sixty soldiers and their families plus the natives from the nearby *ranchería* provided plenty of manpower to construct buildings during the two weeks that the entire expedition remained in San Buenaventura. On April 24, 1782, at Santa Barbara, Neve wrote the Commanding General that the Mission of San Buenaventura had been founded on March 31st, and that by April 12th, there was a complete enclosure of the area of the mission site. The stockade of palings, or limbs of trees set in trenches, woven together with branches or reeds and then daubed with mud, was 50 *varas* long (137 feet) by 40 *varas* wide (110 feet) and 4 *varas* high (11 feet). It had two *revellines*, or bastions (probably placed at diagonally opposite corners), a gate and a small storehouse of palings for provisions. He reported that the site was excellent, with abundant land, wood and stone, and that there was plenty of

[18]Beilharz, *Neve*, pp. 154-55.
[19]Bancroft, *California*, I, 326.

water, the removal of which (from the river by an aqueduct) was assured. He also wrote that the natives were pleased that the settlement was being established.[20]

With work at San Buenaventura well advanced, on April 15, 1782, Neve and all but fifteen of the soldiers with their families set out from San Buenaventura to found Santa Barbara. Neve had left Sergeant Pablo Antonio Cota in charge of fourteen soldiers to protect the mission establishment and build the mission structures. The trip to Santa Barbara, a distance of about twenty-seven miles, was made without incident in one day. Considering that there were women and children to slow the pace and that they were travelling on a rough trail and on the beach, this must have been an exhausting day. In 1769, the Portolá expedition, with no women or children, had taken four days to travel the same terrain.

Except for the officers, most of the participants in the procession were illiterate, so we do not have an account of this trip. We know that west of Ventura much of the first ten miles was along the shoreline where there is almost no flat area between the hills and the surf and where during later decades the wagons, horses and stage coaches traveled through the surf to reach Santa Barbara. We can assume that the entire route followed closely that of the Portolá expedition, and that when they arrived in Santa Barbara, they encamped close to where the presidio was soon founded, near what is now the intersection of Santa Barbara and Canon Perdido streets.

We can also be sure that the site of the temporary encampment was surrounded by open space that would not provide cover for an Indian attack. Although up until then the natives had seemed friendly, Neve, as a military commander, would have taken all precautions to safeguard his charges against a

---

[20]Provincial Record, II, 277-79.

surprise attack by posting sentries and choosing a defensible position. While Father Serra contributed his opinions as to the suitability of various locations for the permanent site of the presidio and mission, it was the Governor who made the final decision, bearing in mind the various factors that will be discussed in this chapter.

As previously stated, Neve had decided in 1777 that the Santa Barbara Presidio should be located midway between San Buenaventura and Point Concepción. This was the section of California's coastline most vulnerable to possible landing and settlement by a foreign power or to severance of communication between the northern and southern settlements by hostile Indians. He had expressed his partiality for the Mescaltitán area, but recognized the need for further reconnaissance before making a final decision. Between April 15, when the expedition arrived at Santa Barbara (it was being called Santa Barbara now instead of Laguna de la Concepción), and April 21, when the presidio was founded, he and his staff surveyed the entire area to appraise the assets and disadvantages of various sites.

Mission sites could be selected by priests, but a decision as to the best location of a presidio needed the knowledge and experience of a soldier. Being a breveted (receiving a rank higher than that for which he receives pay) colonel and having thirty-six years of military experience, Governor Neve was the logical person to select the site for the presidio. He had to weigh numerous factors in his search. From a variety of sources, including statements made with respect to choosing sites for missions, one comes up with the following analysis of his requirements, deliberations and conclusions.

TRANSPORTATION. General Croix had already expressed the need for an anchorage where heavy equipment such as the two cannon could be unloaded from the ship at a point close to the presidio. Neve had requested delivery of supplies to the Channel site by the supply ship from San Blas if the garrison had arrived at the site. Failure to find a suitable landing place would have meant that the cannon and other heavy equipment might have to be transported by land all the way from San Diego, an undertaking to be avoided if at all possible. Cargos had to be hauled on muleback or in *carretas*, the primitive carts with huge wooden wheels fashioned by cutting slices through the trunk of a sycamore tree.

It was essential, therefore, that the presidio be located reasonably near a protected harbor. Ideally, the anchorage should have a sandy bottom where an anchor would hold in rough weather, but that could not be determined by a reconnaissance on land. Croix had urged that Lt. Choquet's visit to the coastline in the *Príncipe* be repeated so that this detail could be determined, but that was not possible prior to the founding.

On his previous trips along the Channel, Neve had probably written off Cojo Bay, Gaviota, Refugio, El Capitán and Carpinteria as having insufficient shelter, leaving only Goleta and Santa Barbara as potential anchorages.[21] The configuration of the coastline at Goleta is similar to that at Santa Barbara, a sharp indentation on the westerly side of the bay flattening out without a promontory on the east side. But the hills back of City College on the west side of the bay at Santa Barbara offer more protection from southwest winds than the mesa on which the University of California, Santa Barbara, is located west of the bay at Goleta.

According to the log of the *Princesa*, the water in the Goleta *estero* surrounding Mescaltitán Island in 1782 was

---

[21]Later all these coves were used, with or without wharves, for shipping out hides, tallow and farm produce, and for the unloading of supplies, lumber, etc. Refugio in particular has an interesting history as a smuggler's port, first when Yankee captains were prohibited from legitimate trade with the Californios, and more recently during prohibition days.

two fathoms deep (twelve feet).[22] The sandbar apparently existed two hundred years ago judging by the description in the log:

> We found the bay to be not at all suitable to come to anchor in it for awhile, as had been thought, as it is very small and has no shelter at all except from the 4th quadrant [northwest], as noted, from a small hill which protects it [the mesa where the University of California, Santa Barbara, is now located], although it has [a depth of] from one to five fathoms of water, the bottom [being] sand, from the seaweed to the land. We likewise examined an opening [into the *estero*] which this small bay had, which at high tide is hardly a fathom and a half [nine feet]; when the tide rises it goes [through the opening in the sandbar] into a large level place which forms a lake which is a mile long, NS [North to South] and in it are two islands, one high [now Mescaltitán Island] and the other flat. The former is greater in circumference. Each one has its large *ranchería*, and they are called Mescaltitán.
>
> I embarked in the boat and went in through the mouth of it [the *estero*] which still had water because the tide had risen. Inside the mouth (which is muddy) we sounded 2 fathoms [12 feet] of water, and afterwards it continued to diminish...

POPULATION DISTRIBUTION. One of the primary purposes of a presidio was to protect the mission establishments so that the missionaries could devote their time to Christianizing the Indians, civilizing them and making them loyal subjects of the King. To accomplish these goals, the missions had to be as close to the center of the native population as possible, which meant that the presidio also should be in that general location to provide maximum protection to the mission establishment.

It has been estimated that the population along the mainland Channel shore during the last quarter of the eighteenth century was about 7,000, although one source estimates as high as 20,000.[23] Historic records give the population of the

---

[22]Sahyun (trans.) and Whitehead (ed.), *Voyage of the Princesa*, p. 69.
[23]Brown, *Aboriginal Population*, p. 79.

village at Burton Mound in Santa Barbara as 500 to 600 persons, and of those around the Goleta Slough as 1,500 to 2,000.[24] Certainly the heaviest concentration was at modern-day Goleta, which would, as a consequence, have been the site most advantageous to the mission. From the standpoint of the presidio, however, proximity to a large Indian population would have been a definite disadvantage because of thefts, for which the Chumash had gained a reputation, and ease of attack.

WATER. Recognizing that any site might be subject to siege, a readily accessible and reliable source of water was a necessity, and one of the first things Neve would look for. Five major creeks empty into the ocean at Goleta. First, however, they empty into the *estero*, or slough, which in the late 1770s extended east-west for a distance of three and a half miles. Therefore, the presidio would have had to be located along the perimeter of the *estero* next to one of the creeks. Neve probably knew that these creeks dried up by April, as they do now.

In the Santa Barbara area, Mission Creek probably flowed all year at that time, and he may have seen the possibility of a dam to provide irrigation and drinking water. Apparently, however, the spring feeding the lake at what is now Garden and Cota streets convinced Neve that a site near it but at a higher elevation, and far enough away from the Indian village at what is now Chapala and Mason streets, would be suitable.

ISOLATION AND TOPOGRAPHY. A site on the shoreline was not acceptable, since foreign ships with cannon having a range exceeding that of the fort's cannon could batter the fort to pieces. Instead, each of the presidios was constructed at a distance of up to a mile from the water, except for San Fran-

---

[24]Brown, *Aboriginal Population*, pp. 29-36.

cisco which had an elaborate *castillo*, or emplaced battery of guns, at a higher elevation which commanded the entrance to the Bay. At San Diego, the presidio was three miles from the ocean and one mile from the bay, and it had a *castillo* at the entrance to the bay. At Monterey, the presidio was 2,000 feet from the shore of the bay on an *estero*. It, too, was protected by a *castillo* at a higher elevation covering the sea approach to the presidio.

The site in Santa Barbara chosen by Neve was isolated from the Indian villages and from the shoreline of the bay, approximately one mile away. Engineering profiles of Santa Barbara and Canon Perdido streets made before those streets were first graded and paved show that there was a small hill on the gradual slope to the ocean at the site of the presidio. The elevation is reflected in the height of the walls of sandstone boulders at the back sides of the sidewalks near the intersection of these two streets. The height of the hill was accentuated by the fact that the topography drops suddenly between Santa Barbara and Garden streets. From the presidio, the soldiers could maintain surveillance over the entire terrain east of Santa Barbara Street clear to what is now Milpas Street, as well as all the way to the shoreline of the bay. It could not be fired upon from a higher elevation as was the case at San Diego and as might have been the case for any site west of Mission Creek in Santa Barbara. The *estero*, which extended from what is now Santa Barbara Street to Milpas Street and as far inland as the Santa Barbara High School and received the waters of Mission Creek, was a marsh area constituting a natural barrier against surprise attack from the east.

In the Goleta area, the Presidio could have been located on More Mesa or on the site of Isla Vista and the University of California, Santa Barbara, but both sites would have been vulnerable to attack from ships at sea. Farther inland there were few elevated sites close enough to the opening in the bluffs at Goleta Slough. Also, the restricted view through this opening prevented sighting of ships approaching from the Channel.

CONSTRUCTION MATERIALS. The essential building materials were wood, stone, adobe and lime. Wood for construction purposes was in short supply, although there was plenty of oak and sycamore firewood for heating, cooking, heating lime to make quicklime and for the kilns to make *tejas* (roof tiles) and *ladrillos* (floor tiles). There was an ample supply of seashells at the Indian villages along the seashore to make quicklime. Adobe soil, of course, was available almost everywhere, although in some locations the quality was not the best for high-strength adobe blocks. Stone was found in quantity on the slopes surrounding the Santa Barbara plain, along the creeks from the foothills to the ocean, and along the shoreline after winter storms had stripped away the sand. In the Goleta Valley, the distance to usable stone apparently was considered excessive.

In a letter to Gálvez from General Croix dated August 26, 1782, Neve is reported to have picked Santa Barbara instead of Mescaltitán (Goleta area) because "besides the advantages of the land, the grass and lumber, stones and water, the last three of which were missing in the second place [Goleta], the chosen site at Santa Barbara is less than a quarter of a league (3,500 feet) from the only sheltered place along the coast that is suitable for anchoring ships."[25]

FERTILITY OF THE SOIL. Due to its distance from the other three presidios and the nine missions, and from the supply depot of San Blas, it was essential that the Santa Barbara settlement produce at least some of its own food. The *Reglamento* of 1781, written by Neve, states that each pre-

---

[25]Junípero Serra Collection 911, dated August 26, 1782.

sidio should have "a drove of twenty-four to thirty mules to carry cargos from the ships, supply provisions for the escorts and aid the presidio which, through the loss or considerable delay of a vessel, might be lacking in grain and articles of the first importance." They would also be needed for the "other tasks which must be performed in establishing the presidio and missions in the pass of Santa Barbara Channel... During the first year all goods must be carried by land," and afterward, the mules would be needed to convey "the produce of the pueblos to the presidio."[26]

A primary function of the pueblos in the colonization plan was to have the settlers raise food to supply the presidios. Later, the missions had to supply food for the presidios because the pueblos did not produce enough.

Father Junípero Serra was not at all happy about Governor Neve's decision regarding the site of the presidio, but it must be kept in mind that Serra expected the mission to be located adjacent to the presidio. In a letter dated July 17, 1782, to Father Guardian Pangua of the College of San Fernando in Mexico City, Serra wrote:

> On the 15th [of April 1782] I set out [from San Buenaventura] in company with His Lordship [Neve] for the Santa Barbara district...On the same day...we came to the site that His Lordship had selected for the Santa Barbara Presidio. In my humble opinion it was suitable neither for a presidio nor for a mission.
>
> I really have not the heart to describe to you what a sorry sight that foundation presents, nor to tell you all that I saw and heard during the three weeks I stayed in that district. The Governor was acting as a missionary. He says that we do not have the gift for it, and he promised to give Father Cambón the formula for it.[27]

The letter was written after Serra learned that founding of the Santa Barbara Mission was to be delayed, which may

---

[26]Johnson (trans.), *Regulations for Governing*, Title One, Section 7, p. 6.
[27]Tibesar, *Writings of Serra*, IV, 151-53.

have soured him regarding Santa Barbara in general. But he was also upset with the way the Governor was treating him and interfering in the missionary program.

From the foregoing analysis, we can conclude that the site along the Channel was picked to prevent severance of the line of communication by land between the northern and southern settlements and because of the high density of the Indian population. Neve chose the Santa Barbara location because it had the best nearby anchorage; it offered a reasonably good supply of water, stone and wood; the Indians were friendly; the soil was fertile; and irrigation works were feasible.

Perhaps Neve was impressed by the beauty of the area. He may have noted that living in such an equable climate would make life easier for his soldiers. In reality, Santa Barbara was founded purely for military strategic reasons. The specific site was chosen because of distance from the main Indian village, proximity to the lagoon, elevation above surrounding land which provided a view of incoming ships and possible attack by hostile Indians, good drainage in wet weather and because it was close enough to shore for transporting supplies delivered by ship yet far enough away to be out of the cannon-reach of enemy ships. None of these factors, with the exception of good drainage, is an important consideration in choosing sites for modern developments.

Figure 2: Russell A. Ruiz sketch of the Santa Barbara
Presidio founding ceremony.

Chapter Five

Founding and Initial Construction

Governor Neve's report of April 24, 1782, to the Commanding General of the Internal Provinces concerning the
founding of the Santa Barbara Presidio was paraphrased
from the original by one of Bancroft's scribes. It reads:

> On the 15th of the current month he arrived at this place called
> previously *San Joaquín de la Laguna* and found that its lake pro-
> vided an abundant supply of good water, much wood, and stone,
> and at less than a quarter league from the only anchoring ground
> known in the Channel, sufficient wood and pasture lands. The Pre-
> sidio of Santa Barbara was located on this site on the 11th [sic] of
> the current month, enhancing its position at a small rise next to the
> lake. Immediately they began the cutting of paling to enclose an
> area of sixty *varas* [165 feet] with two *revellines* [bastions] of oak
> which will serve while they complete the actual structure which
> will be eighty *varas* [220 feet] square with two small bastions.
> There remains to be constructed a stretch of paling whose cutting
> and transporting will probably delay the completion because the
> palings are so thick, even though eight teams of oxen work until the
> middle of May. But in its class, it will be the strongest. He
> exchanged presents with Yananalit, [sic] captain of the large
> *ranchería* which is next to the beach and the required landing place.
> They [the natives] have come to see it and he told the captains he
> would let them know the day on which each one of their people
> might come to visit it, a precaution which he has taken to avoid too
> many people [at one time] which at present is not proper. He never
> expected the submissiveness of these Gentiles, who he believes are
> twice as many as those which he calculated before, counting only

twenty-one *rancherías,* and it is now evident there are many more who populate the foot of the Sierra.[1]

From Father Junípero Serra we obtain a more detailed description of the founding ceremonies. A letter to the same Commanding General dated April 28, 1782, reads in part:

> We arrived here at the Santa Barbara Channel on April 15. We spent some time in talking over which would be the best site for the foundation, then in getting everything in readiness. And so, the very next Sunday, which was the third Sunday after Easter and the feast day of the Patronage of the Most Holy Patriarch Saint Joseph, the foundation was started. There were all the usual ceremonies - the setting up and blessing of a large Cross, the blessing of the site, the first Mass, with an accompanying sermon. And so was begun this presidio and mission—at present they are united in one—dedicated to the most glorious Virgin and Martyr Santa Barbara.[2]

Serra wrote a similar letter to Fr. Lasuén on the 29th in which he states that the founding occurred "in the land of Yamnonalit" (see figure 2). He adds, "I was all alone here, and still am, and for that reason we could have only a low Mass; and instead of singing the *Te Deum* we substituted the *Alabado,* or *Laudamus.* Serra wrote at the end of the letter "Mission-Presidio of Santa Barbara."[3] Obviously, up to April 29th, Serra thought he had founded the mission of Santa Barbara at the same time as the Santa Barbara Presidio was started.

Tibesar writes that Father Serra left Santa Barbara to

---

[1] Provincial Records, II, 278-79. The scribe evidently erred, copying April 11th instead of April 21st. The expedition was in Ventura on the 11th. His reference to villages at the foot of the Sierra was to villages in the Santa Ynez Valley.

[2] Tibesar, *Writings of Serra,* IV, 135.

[3] Tibesar, *Writings of Serra,* IV, 141. Yamnonalit, spelled various ways in the documentation, was the name of the chief of the Indian village at *Shuktu* located on a small hill (Burton Mound) that became the site of the Potter Hotel near Stearn's Wharf. His name, modified to Yanonali, was later given to a street on the east side of Santa Barbara.

return to Monterey about May 5th.[4] Sometime between April 29th and May 5th, one to six days after the founding ceremonies, Governor Neve told Serra that the founding of the mission had not occurred and that it was to be delayed indefinitely. Neve must have known on April 21st that he was not going to approve the founding of the mission. His reason could not have been the massacre at Yuma in July of 1781. That had happened nearly a year before, and he had not countermanded the founding of San Buenaventura Mission. Both Engelhardt and Beilharz have concluded that Neve's opposition to the old system of housing Indians at the mission rather than allowing them to remain in their villages accounted for his decision. In this writer's opinion, Neve's action was pure vindictiveness brought about by his long-standing resentment and frustration over Serra's independence from governmental regulations and his success in getting his own way. If this conclusion is correct, it is an indication of the clout exercised by the religious at the higher echelons of government.

No record has been found of the names of the people present at the ceremonies for the founding of the presidio. We know that fifty-seven officers and men left San Gabriel and that Sergeant Pablo Cota and fourteen men were left at San Buenaventura to construct the mission and protect the priests.[5] There should have been forty-two soldiers of the Santa Barbara garrison at the founding of the Presidio of Santa Barbara, plus Neve and his escort, Father Serra, mission servants and neophyte interpreters. By consulting the marriage, death and baptismal records at Mission San Buenaventura and Mission Santa Barbara, a list of those who probably were at the founding ceremonies has been developed.

---

[4]Tibesar, *Writings of Serra,* IV, 439, fn. 73.
[5]Provincial State Papers, Benicia Military, III, 106-08.

Between April 21, 1782, the founding date of the presidio, and December 4, 1786, the founding date of Santa Barbara Mission, the ceremonies of baptism and marriage took place at San Buenaventura because there was no resident priest at Santa Barbara. In many cases, the marriage and baptismal record indicates that the soldier was "of the *escolta* of San Buenaventura Mission." If a soldier died at Santa Barbara, the priest would have had to travel up from San Buenaventura to perform the burial ceremony, and the record would show that the soldier was buried at Santa Barbara. An error would occur if a member of the San Buenaventura *escolta* was on temporary duty at Santa Barbara when he died.[6] If a soldier or one of his family was listed in the San Buenaventura burial register, it is assumed the soldier was a member of the San Buenaventura *escolta*. Again, an error would occur if the soldier was on temporary duty at San Buenaventura.

On April 21, 1782, six days after arriving at Santa Barbara, the founding ceremonies were held. That same day, Father Serra wrote the title page for two registers he had brought with him, those for baptisms and for deaths. In both registers, he wrote "this new mission and royal presidio." When the Mission of Santa Barbara was finally founded December 4, 1786, Fr. Fermín Lasuén scratched out the words "mission and" and inserted at the bottom of the page a statement explaining that founding of the mission was delayed for more than four years and was located at a distance of half a league to the northeast (see figure 3). For that reason the registers were restricted to entries occurring at the presidio, another book being opened for entries at the mission.

On June 2, 1782, Governor Neve made an inspection of the Santa Barbara Presidio and reported on his findings to Commanding General Croix. Just five and a half weeks after

---

[6]The Santa Barbara Mission Archive-Library has copies of the baptismal, death and confirmation registers of almost all the California missions.

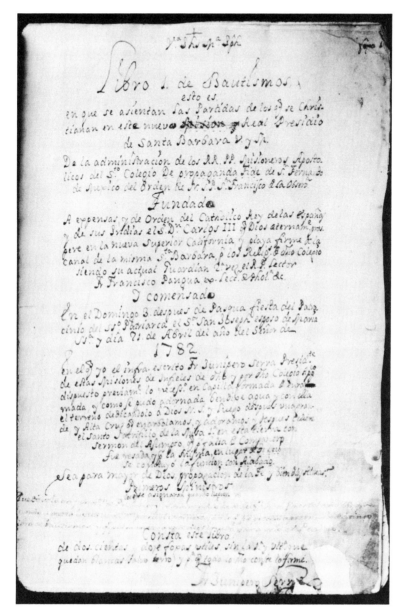

Figure 3: Title page of Baptismal Register for Santa Barbara Presidio.
Courtesy Santa Barbara Mission Archive-Library.

the founding, Neve reported that the plastering, flat roofs, storehouse, guardhouse and barracks remained to be finished and that the natives were still happy about the Spanish settlement.[7] The troops were put through the manual of arms, cavalry formations and target practice, and performed satisfactorily in spite of the fact of their recent recruitment and the large amount of time they had spent on constructing the presidio. The Governor was complimentary of Lt. Ortega on most counts, but said he had to reprimand him for being too familiar with the troops. He also lacked firmness and determination, and his accounts as paymaster were in such bad shape, in spite of his known intelligence in such matters, that Neve recommended he be quickly replaced. He said that if Ortega continued as paymaster the inevitable result would be bankruptcy. Neve considered him a good officer under the direction of another commander.

Uniforms were in deplorable shape because the shipment of supplies from San Blas for 1782 had not yet arrived. However, Neve had received word that the supply ships *Princesa* and *Favorita* were at the port of Monterey. The Governor reported on the status of armament, powder, cartridges and the horses and mules. Much of the equipment was defective. The safeties on the pistols were inoperative and the swords of Toledo steel were tempered so highly that they would break into pieces if used carelessly.[8] (One wonders just how "careless use" of a sword was defined.)

A letter from Neve to Ortega dated June 30, 1782, gives instructions for the unloading of supplies from the frigates *Princesa* and *Favorita* when they arrived at Santa Barbara. A guard was to be posted to watch the merchandise and to prevent the sailors from molesting the Indians. Neve anticipated

---

[7]Provincial Record, II, 281.

[8]*Archivo General de la Nación, Audiencia de Guadalajara, legajo* 518 (microfilm reel 1806 in Bancroft Library, p. 14). The document was dated December 30, 1782.

the curiosity of the natives, who had never seen a ship unload its cargo in their bay. Whoever was in charge of the guard was to make a record of every package, box, barrel and basket. Goods from Mexico, with their marks on the front, were to be stored in the warehouse; the others, presumably anything from San Francisco or Monterey, were to go in the store-house. The difference between these two buildings is not explained, but probably the storehouse was the building where provisions and other supplies could be purchased by the soldiers and their families.

Seeds were not to be mixed with those belonging to the missions. They were to be placed in coverings so that they would not be spoiled by dampness from the ground or walls. No package or box was to be opened without an order from a superior, and if there were any differences in the weights and measures from the order, a record was to be made so that cer-tification could be filed.[9]

One report regarding the attitude of the Santa Barbara natives to the intrusion of the Spanish is missing from avail-able documents written by Neve, but appears in a letter from Croix to Gálvez dated August 26, 1782. It reads in part:

> In its neighborhood are numerous *rancherías* of Captain Yananolit, who at the beginning did not like the location of the presidio, but persuaded by Governor Felipe de Neve who knew him, expressed his pleasure and gave that official some baskets and other things in token of his esteem, so that he had to admit to seeing the Indians very sensitive to [accepting] what had been contrary to their wishes.

Neve also says in another official letter of June 6 that Yananolit is chief of the *rancherías* and the most powerful and feared of the Channel, and that his people were at war with those of Mescaltitán, and they have become reconciled at his instance; and finally that "all the pagans are apparently happy

---

[9]Provincial State Papers, III, 83-85.

and tranquil and pleased that we have established ourselves in their country; in spite of which one lives in the new presidio whose defense works are being hastened forward with corresponding precaution."[10]

At 3 P.M. on August 1, 1782, soldiers at the presidio heard the booming of cannon coming from the west. In these days of urban noise generated by airplanes, railroad trains and highway traffic, the sound of cannon-fire travelling a distance of ten miles seems almost unbelievable. By prearrangement, in a letter we do not have, the soldiers sent up a smoke signal which was seen by the sailors on the frigate *Princesa*, which was anchored beyond the kelp bed outside of the bay at Goleta.[11] The ships had a dual responsibility: to deliver the first load of supplies from the depot at San Blas to the new Santa Barbara Presidio, and to map the ports and coastline in its vicinity so that other ships could safely identify landmarks and navigate to the new settlement.

In the year-end strength report required of each company, Ortega listed himself as commanding officer, Josef Argüello as his *alférez*, or ensign, in addition to Sergeants Pablo Cota and Josef Olivares, Corporals Alejandro de Soto and Josef de Ortega and fifty soldiers.[12] Fifteen were in the *escolta* at San Buenaventura, seven at San Luis Obispo on a temporary assignment and two were in Los Angeles. This left thirty-two men at Santa Barbara available for duty, not a large force to defend from foreign encroachment the two hundred miles of coastline between Los Angeles and Morro Bay or protect Santa Barbara from an attack by hostile Indians.

Some events of importance to the new settlement occurred in 1783. A letter dated January 10, 1783, from

---

[10]Junípero Serra Collection, 911, in Santa Barbara Mission Archive-Library.

[11]Sahyun (trans.) and Whitehead (ed.), *Voyage of the Princesa*, p. 63. The voyage of the two frigates, the *Favorita* and the *Princesa*, from San Blas to San Francisco, Monterey, Santa Barbara and San Diego is described in great detail in this book.

[12]Provincial State Papers, Benicia Military, IV, 159.

Nicolás Soler, Inspector of California troops, to Lt. Diego Gonzales, commanding officer of the Monterey garrison, authorized fabrication of a brand for the horses and mules of each of the presidios (see figure 4).

Figure 4:

Presidio	Date of Founding	Livestock Brand
Loreto	October 25, 1697	(brand: A)
San Diego	July 16, 1769	(brand: 2A)
Monterey	June 3, 1770	(brand: A3)
San Francisco	September 17, 1776	(brand: 4A)
Santa Barbara	April 21, 1782	(brand: 5A)

The "A" after the number is probably for the last letter of the words *primera*, *segunda*, *tercera*, *quarta* and *quinta compañía* and the numbers represent the order in which the various presidios were founded.[13]

---

[13]Provincial State Papers, Benicia Military, V, 166. When this author encountered the document at The Bancroft Library, he thought he had, exclusively, a new bit of presidio information. On a visit to the plaza at San Juan Bautista, however, the listings were noted thumbtacked to the wall of the livery stable. The brands make an interesting logo for modern works on the various presidios.

Governor Neve lost no time in arranging for a replacement for Lt. Ortega as commander at Santa Barbara. Don Felipe Antonio de Goycoechea was promoted from *alférez* (ensign) to lieutenant January 14, 1783, with orders to assume command of the Santa Barbara Company.[14] For various reasons, the actual takeover did not occur for another year.

New presidial commander Goycoechea, of Basque descent, had been born in 1747 in the Real de Cosalá, a small town ninety miles southeast of Culiacán in the province of Sinaloa.[15] His service began as a *cadete* on June 1, 1782, six weeks after the founding of the Santa Barbara Presidio. He was at the Presidio of Fronteras, southeast of Tucson, for two weeks, then was promoted to *alférez* and sent to the Presidio of Buena Vista in southern Sonora, Mexico. After nearly seven months at that presidio, he was transferred to the Presidio of Loreto and commanded that installation for a year before taking over at Santa Barbara. The explanation for Goycoechea's rapid promotions and his activities before entering military service must wait until someone researches his life history. We know that his promotions must have been deserved, since he remained as the commanding officer of the Santa Barbara Presidio from 1784 until 1802 and was then Governor of Baja California for eight years. He was a bachelor, but while at Santa Barbara, fathered a boy by the widow of one of the presidio soldiers.

A clue to his rapid promotion lies in the fact that he entered the service as a *cadete*. According to historian Marc Simmons, cadets were young men, usually the sons of officers, who received their appointments directly from the viceroy or the commanding general.[16] They served in the

---

[14]Provincial Record, II, 272.

[15]*Archivo General de Simancas*, GM 7278C9

[16]Simmons, *Spanish Government in New Mexico*, p. 116.

ranks, but did not live with the soldiers, associating with the officers. They received only a soldier's pay, so to live and dress like an officer, they had to have an independent income. Obviously, Goycoechea's family were not peasants.

Goycoechea prepared and signed a map of the Santa Barbara Presidio dated in 1788 which will be described later, but there is a mystery about several entries in the record regarding a plan in 1783. A brief memo from the blotter or daily correspondence record of Pedro Fages to Commanding General Croix dated March 1783 states that Fages is sending a plan of the Santa Barbara Presidio.[17] A letter from Fages to Ortega dated May 23, 1783, tells why he could not have sent him the plan of the presidio except by his courier, but the scribe omits the reason.[18]

A document dated August 25, 1783, from Felipe de Neve to Pedro Fages, as translated from the notes of Bancroft's scribe, reads: "He says that he has in his possession the plan which he has made for the construction of the Presidio of Santa Barbara and that he is trying to push it forward…"[19] A blotter entry dated January 7, 1784, reads "on approval of the plan of the Presidio," referring to a document received by Ortega.[20]

The mystery of this "plan," whether it is the one dated September 16, 1788, of which we have a copy, or another plan which has not yet surfaced, or whether the "plan" is simply a program for construction of the presidio rather than a drawing, will not be solved until the original documents summarized by Bancroft's scribes are found. The local copies were probably destroyed in the 1906 San Francisco fire, but

---

[17]Provincial Record, III, 177.
[18]Provincial Record, III, 103.
[19]State Papers—Sacramento, XV, 287.
[20]Provincial State Papers, V, 221.

copies may exist in Mexico City or Seville, waiting to be discovered.

More information on the activities of the Santa Barbara Company during 1782 and 1783 has not been unearthed. In August 1782, Fages and Neve set out for a rendezvous on the Colorado River to mount a campaign against the Yuma Indians in retaliation for the massacre of July 1781.[21] En route, on September 4, 1782, Neve received word from Croix that he (Neve) had been promoted to Inspector General of the Internal Provinces. Fages, appointed Governor of the Californias as a result, returned to Monterey. Neve went on to start the war against the Yumas, but put them to flight in one skirmish and that ended the war, though it can hardly be considered a Spanish victory since control was never reestablished over the Colorado River groups.

Interest in establishing the Santa Barbara Mission occupied Fages's attention, and a document dated December 5, 1783, from him to the Commanding General reports that Fages, accompanied by Fr. Vicente de Santa María, then stationed at San Buenaventura, examined the place called "Montecito, one league to the south of Santa Barbara and three valleys in length. It is thought to be a proper place to establish the mission."[22] A report dated August 1, 1784, from Fages to the Commanding General records Fages's approval for the founding of the Santa Barbara Mission in Montecito.[23] Subsequently, however, the site, which may have been in the vicinity of what is now San Ysidro Road and East Valley Road, was inspected by Goycoechea and Fr. Lasuén and found to be unsuitable.

On January 25, 1784, Lt. Ortega handed over command of the Santa Barbara Presidio to Lt. Felipe de Goycoechea.[24] As is still the custom in military organizations when a change of command occurs, an inventory was made of all the equip-

---

[21]Beilharz, *Neve*, pp. 127-28.   [22]Provincial Record, III, 186.

[23]Provincial Record, I, 180.   [24]Provincial Record, I, 163.

ment, supplies, provisions, clothing, arms, ammunition, horses, mules, etc., so that the outgoing officer could be relieved of all future responsibility. This document has not been found, but inventories of some of the items plus other informative documents do exist to help us visualize how the presidio looked when Goycoechea assumed command.

We have no description of what the palisade-type buildings at Santa Barbara looked like other than what appears in the orders to Ortega. Except for the fact that Santa Barbara had no pine, redwood or cypress trees, the best description so far, but applicable to the buildings of Carmel Mission south of Monterey, was written in a letter from Serra to Fr. Rafael Verger, Guardian of San Fernando College, dated August 8, 1772:

> The principal building has a flat roof of clay and dirt. The walls are made of stout limbs of pine trees, stripped off and well trimmed, the spaces in between filled with stones, rubble or branches and stuccoed all over both inside and out. The roof is made of thick beams of both pine and cypress well trimmed, and covered with poles and straw protected by plastered clay and mud. The said house is fifteen yards wide and fifty and a half long, divided into six rooms, that is, three cells, two of them with alcoves, an office, a reception room, and also a granary or storehouse...
>
> One of the cells serves as a church until the day when a separate church with a sacristy can be built, in a place selected for that purpose.
>
> The four rooms, that is the reception room, the cells and provisional church, are whitewashed with lime inside, and all of them can be entered from inside, thus making a number of doorways necessary...Some of these doors are made of pine boards, others of cypress, and others again of a red wood whose name we do not know, but which is from a fine and noble tree...
>
> The said house is furnished with water jars, a bookcase, scissor-shaped seats, some covered with woven reeds, others with leather; two large benches, one larger than the other, two tables, cupboards, etc.[25]

---

[25]Tibesar, *Writings of Serra*, I, 255-57.

Another letter, written May 21, 1773, to Viceroy Bucareli, gives more information about the Carmel Mission installation:

> The first thing we put our hands to in the new location was, as is usual, the palisade and our living quarters. In the case of both we had the great advantage, over the others, that nature favored the place with an abundance of timber of various kinds, all close at hand. And here the soldiers were most devoted to the work. May God reward them!
>
> The enclosure of the palisade is made of stout poles, close to one another, and of considerable height, with their *revellines* at the corners; the length is a little more than seventy yards and the depth forty-three. At night it is closed with lock and key. But because it is not firmly nailed together—we did not possess any nails—an entrance can easily be effected by knocking down or pushing aside some of the poles.
>
> The main building is seven yards in width and fifty in length...The walls made of stout poles are plastered inside and out, and the principal rooms are whitewashed with lime...
>
> Near the palisade, but outside of it, is the guardhouse or soldiers' quarters, and near it their kitchen; both have their palisade around them.
>
> All of these buildings have their flat roofs of clay and earth. In addition to these, our kitchen was built, and various little structures for the Indians, thatched with straw and brush.[26]

Conditions were quite different at Santa Barbara. Timbers suitable for construction close to the presidio site were non-existent. The defense wall of palings would have had to be built of alders, small sycamores and willows. To bind them together, they used willow branches and reeds. Clay and mud would have been the plastering materials and sea shells the source of lime. There were some outcroppings of lime, but it is doubtful they had been discovered at this early date. Perhaps the soldiers copied a technique seen in the Indian huts, using reeds woven together to thatch the flat roofs. The roofs

---

[26]Tibesar, *Writings of Serra*, I, 351-53.

would have given them the greatest problem, because in a driving rain any flat roofs using mud and clay to shed the water would have dribbled mud down into the room.

No record has been found that adobe blocks were made during the period when Ortega was in command. We can assume that by November 1782, six months after the founding, when the rains probably began, the buildings were all as watertight as they would ever be, and the defense wall enclosed the quadrangle to give them a sense of security.

The Indians had turned out to be quite friendly, and they were even employed in the construction work, being paid in food and trinkets. The supplies that arrived on the *Princesa* and *Favorita* were safely sheltered in buildings, providing adequate food, clothing and other provisions until arrival of the supply ships in the late summer of 1783. A letter dated February 10, 1784, from Governor Fages to the Commanding General reports that the water taken from the stony creek (Mission Creek was first called *Pedregoso* or Stony Creek) runs in front of the gate in abundance and permanently. Obviously, Ortega had had a ditch, or possibly a stone-lined aqueduct, built from some dam along Mission Creek to the Presidio two years prior to the founding of the Mission. Fr. Maynard Geiger, Archivist at the Santa Barbara Mission Archive-Library from 1937 to his death in 1977, discovered a letter from Neve to Gálvez dated October 20, 1783, which states:

> The numerous Indians who inhabit the said Channel remain quiet and tranquil, and according to the latest news I have received from the said Ortega, they have gladly and voluntarily labored on the buildings of the presidio and the aqueduct constructed from the source of the Pedregozo, distant a quarter of a league [two thirds of a mile], to bring water to the presidio's very walls facing its principal entrance.[27]

---

[27]Geiger, *Life and Times of Serra*, II, 289-90.

In quoting this letter, Father Geiger inserted the words "the *salto de agua* (waterfall or fountain)" after the word "walls." These words do not appear in the original letter obtained from the Newberry Library in Chicago. Evidently Father Geiger assumed that the aqueduct terminated in a fountain or washing trough where women could wash their clothes, as exists at the Santa Barbara Mission. This is a logical assumption, since such a facility would be essential at the presidio.

Father Geiger once told this writer that he had seen the stone-lined aqueduct leading to the presidio along the southerly right-of-way line of Laguna Street from near the Mission fountain to Los Olivos Street. The probable alignment of the aqueduct from there to the presidio has been plotted using large-scale topographic maps in the hope that some day a crew of volunteers would accept precising of the alignment as a research project. They would have to contact property owners along the alignment to determine if a stone aqueduct had ever been uncovered on their property. Russell A. Ruiz and Pearl Chase discovered where the aqueduct penetrated the presidio defense wall a few feet north of the intersection of the northeasterly right-of-way line of Santa Barbara Street with the northwesterly boundary of the former Santa Barbara City College property. Unfortunately, no pictures or measurements were taken and funds have not been available to locate the aqueduct by archaeological investigation (see figure 5).[28]

The original watercourse was probably a simple unlined ditch, since it preceded founding of the mission. Later it was

---

[28]On March 15, 1988 a 30-foot long section of the aqueduct was unearthed during archaeological excavation of the *comandancia* site. The portion uncovered extends from the *zaguán* of the *comandancia* diagonally to a point about in the middle of the 900 block of Santa Barbara Street. The bottom of the aqueduct is formed by *ladrillos;* large stones form the sides and cap. The entire structure is held together by Roman cement chinked with smaller stones. *Ed. note.*

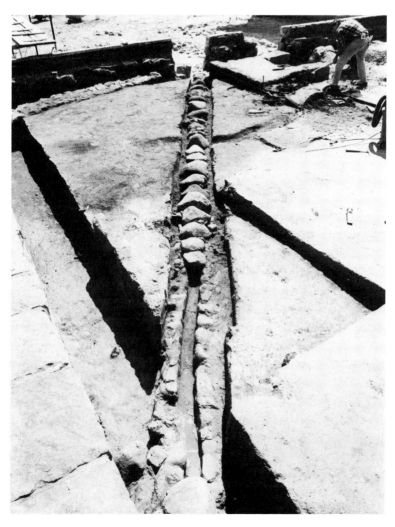

Figure 5: Portion of remaining Santa Barbara Presidio aqueduct discovered in 1989. Photo by Wm. B. Dewey.

lined with *ladrillos* or rocks, as was done for the mission aqueducts in Mission and Las Canoas canyons. Still later a reservoir was built within the presidio quadrangle. The possible floor of this reservoir was discovered by Jeremy Hass, former member of the Board of Trustees of the Trust for Historic Preservation. When utilities in the vicinity of the presidio were being placed underground, there appeared to be a horizontal row of stone along the southeasterly gutter of Canon Perdido Street about fifty feet from the east corner of Canon Perdido and Santa Barbara streets.

The period of initial construction ended with the commencement of permanent building when Felipe de Goycoechea accepted command of the fifth company, the Santa Barbara Royal Presidio garrison. José Francisco Ortega was transferred to Loreto. He applied for retirement in 1786 after thirty years of service, pleading age and obesity, but his request was denied. He continued in the service until he was retired as a brevet captain in 1795, attached to the Santa Barbara Company. He died suddenly on February 3, 1798, at *Casil*, the Indian *ranchería* at the mouth of Refugio Canyon, twenty miles west of Santa Barbara.[29]

---

[29]Bancroft, *California*, I, 670-72.

Chapter Six

Presidio Design

The design of forts has taxed the ingenuity of military engineers and their knowledge of mathematics and physics since the time of the Greeks and Romans. Exterior walls were carefully designed to provide maximum security and minimum chance that the wall would be pierced or crumble under attack. The shape of walls was mathematically designed to make cannon balls ricochet with as little damage to the walls and interior of the fort as possible. Detailed planning and design of military installations has continued as a science to as late as the 1940s when training camps were established in the early stages of World War II.

Originally, a fort was designed to serve two purposes: to provide a sanctuary within which soldiers and their families could live and work safely in a hostile area, and to serve as a defensive position which could withstand attack from the enemy and from which its soldiers could sally forth to attack the enemy. To accomplish these purposes in what was called the Internal Provinces of New Spain, the area between the Gulf of California and the Gulf of Mexico generally along the present boundary between Mexico and the United States, a chain of fifteen presidios was established at intervals of approximately forty leagues, as noted in a previous chapter. These forts were intended to safeguard the lives and estates of the subjects of King Charles III from attacks of the fierce Apache, Comanche and other Indians. They supplemented and protected the activities of the missionaries sent to convert and civilize the Indians.

Spain's efforts to dominate, civilize and exploit the northern reaches of New Spain, commencing with the Coronado expedition in 1540 and extending into the nineteenth century, met with failures, not the least of which were the inadequacies of the presidial system. Lack of training, insufficient incentive, inferior weapons, dishonest and greedy officers, and shortages of supplies and equipment, combined with the far-flung boundaries of the frontiers, were all contributing causes. However, the inability of an emplaced presidio garrison to outmaneuver a band of mounted Indians using guerrilla tactics was a major factor. Guerrilla forces are still able to harass, outwit and in many cases defeat a much stronger enemy.

In the Internal Provinces, it was the practice of the presidio soldiers to pasture their horses at a distance from the fort where grass for grazing was available. A guard of perhaps five soldiers was assigned to camp out with the horses to secure them against attacks by wild animals or hostile natives. The Indians soon learned how easy it was to massacre the guard, drive off the horses, and thus immobilize the entire garrison.

The *Reglamento* of 1772 corrected some of the system's deficiencies. In addition to relocating a number of the presidios to enable better control of the regular travel routes of the Indians, a standard pattern for the design of the presidio was established:

> The exterior walls are to be built first of adobes, with two small bastions [*baluartes*] in the angles; afterward on the interior will be built the chapel, the guardhouse, residences for the captain, officers, and chaplain, and quarters for the soldiers and Indians, sheltering everyone during the construction in campaign tents and temporary barracks... It is understood that this work should be done by the troops as a campaign task and that it will accrue to their benefit and

protection; the Indian scouts are not to be burdened with more work than that of the soldiers, for both should be treated equally. All should be given a moderate gratuity for this special work.[1]

It is only reasonable to assume that there was a standard layout for a presidio, since many were being constructed in the Internal Provinces and in the Californias, all within a period of a few decades. Each fort would have to be modified to fit the terrain and surrounding topography, but would be based upon a common pattern. That pattern had been developed over centuries of time in Europe and the Mediterranean—a quadrangle enclosed by a defense wall and housing troops and equipment. The wall had various battlements from which the defenders could fire upon the attackers. As will be seen later, the pattern described in the 1772 *Reglamento* was used for the permanent construction of the presidio at Santa Barbara. But who designed the standard? The answer seems to appear in the *Reglamento.*[2] After listing the fifteen presidios to be included on the line of the frontier, this document states that "as shown on the map drawn up by the regular engineer Don Nicolás Lafora, [two are to have] their enclosures strengthened, constructing them according to the plan of the same engineer." If there was no standard plan, at least we know the name of the person who designed some of the presidios.

In conformity with the plan set forth in the 1772 *Reglamento,* some presidios along the northern frontier were abandoned and some were relocated to more strategic sites. According to Faulk, these presidios were similar in design and construction.[3] Usually located near good farming land and on high ground, they were built according to a pattern learned from the Moors. Constructed of local materials

---

[1]Brinckerhoff and Faulk, *Lancers,* p. 63.
[2]Brinckerhoff and Faulk, *Lancers,* p. 49.
[3]Faulk, "The Presidio: Fortress or Farce?" pp. 23-24.

(principally adobe bricks), the presidios were square or rectangular in shape with walls at least ten feet high. The length of the sides ranged from 200 to 800 feet each. On two diagonal corners, round bastions projecting beyond the alignment of the walls were constructed. The parapets of the bastions rose above the wall and were pierced with firing ports for cannon. This arrangement permitted the soldiers to fire down the length of all four walls at attackers who might be attempting to scale the walls. On the inside of the walls, buildings were constructed with roofs high enough to serve as platforms for men firing over the parapet of the defense wall. Included inside the presidio were storage facilities, a chapel, and rooms for the officers and men. The only outside opening was the main gate.

Variations in this basic design involved wooden palisades and diamond-shaped, square or round bastions. At Santa Cruz de Terrenate, southeast of Tucson, there was only one bastion, diamond-shaped.[4] The design of these presidios was so practical that many American traders and military leaders at a later date chose to build their forts in the same pattern.

It was the responsibility of Colonel Hugo O'Conor, an Irish mercenary, to carry out the orders of the *Reglamento* of 1772 under the general supervision of Viceroy Bucareli. Although O'Conor was considered competent, the presidio program remained unsuccessful, and in 1776 the Internal Provinces were removed from the jurisdiction of the viceroy and placed under a commandant-general, Brigadier Teodoro de Croix, with civil, judicial and military powers. Croix's effectiveness was limited, however, by the fact that he was still dependent on the viceroy for troops and supplies.

The ruins of nine of the presidios built under O'Conor between 1772 and 1775 along the northerly frontier of Mex-

---

[4]For detailed archaeological findings see: Di Peso, *The Sobaipuri Indians.*

ico were located and excavated by Rex E. Gerald, and the results of his archaeological research were published in 1968.[5] In summarizing Gerald's work, Max Moorhead states:

> Of these nine presidios, seven were built on a rectangular plan, one (San Vicente) was laid out as a diamond, and the other (San Eleazario) as a quasi-quadrangle with two adjoining plazas. All were completely enclosed, and most or all were constructed of adobe brick, as prescribed by the *Reglamento*. At least three had attached corrals for the horses, which were probably added later as a result of Croix's reforms. All but one of the structures had angular bastions at one or two corners, which constituted the principal distinction between the fortifications built before and after 1772. San Vicente, the lone exception, had one angular bastion and one circular tower. The new bastions were more spacious than the old towers and, being constructed on a diamond-shaped plan, offered superior flanking protection for the walls and gates...
>
> The guardhouses in the new presidios were always situated on either side of the main gate, as in the past, and the captain's quarters was a large block of rooms on the side of the plaza opposite the main gate, while the soldiers' quarters lined the interior of the perimeter wall. These apartments, or rooms, measured only six and a half meters in width and seven in length at San Carlos, close quarters indeed for a soldier and his entire family. [Rooms in the building assigned to soldiers' families in the Santa Barbara Presidio were eight by five *varas* (22 feet by 13.75 feet or 6.7 meters by 4.19 meters), smaller even than those excavated by Gerald.] The number of such rooms did not always correspond to the number of troops in the company, however, for in several cases Indian auxiliaries and even soldiers had to be quartered in huts outside of the compound. The chapel usually had its long axis perpendicular to and midway along the inner side of one of the perimeter walls. Recent excavations indicate that at least some of the interior walls were plastered (at San Eleazario, for instance) first with brown mud and then with one or more layers of whitewash.[6]

[5]Rex E. Gerald, *Spanish Presidios.*
[6]Moorhead, *The Presidio*, pp. 166-67.

Gerald states that the chapels were almost always in the center of the south or west walls and were constructed with their long axis at right angles to the wall. He also points out that although there is no specific mention of them, a magazine (for ammunition), an armory and one or more storage rooms must have been included in the plan for the presidios. The *Reglamento* required that some 350 pounds of powder be kept on hand, as well as a replacement supply of weapons, weapon parts and uniform components.

Our knowledge of the design of the Santa Barbara Presidio far exceeds that of any other presidio in California, as well as in the Southwest, thanks to documents that have been preserved. A document in The Bancroft Library dated September 16, 1788, from Commandant Goycoechea to Governor Fages describes in detail the status of construction on the presidio as of that date. This document was translated by Mrs. Geraldine V. Sahyun in the early 1960s and was a major impetus for much of the archaeology and historical research that commenced in 1967. Incorporated in the document is a plan of the presidio with a number for each building. For each number, there is a description of the use of the building; the length, breadth and height of each room; and the materials of construction for that building or room.[7]

The introductory sentence on this map indicates that it is a statement to Governor Fages, prepared by Goycoechea, showing the present state of construction of the presidio. The copy in The Bancroft Library was traced by Bancroft's scribes on tracing cloth, using both sides of the tracing cloth. As a result, the ink has bled through the cloth and the document is difficult to read.

Knowing of the interest in the Santa Barbara Presidio, Father Charles Polzer, S.J., of the Southwestern Mission

---

[7]Provincial State Papers, XII, 62.

Research Center in Tucson, notified this writer in 1976 that he had found in the Newberry Library a similar map of the presidio with the same date but signed by Governor Fages. This Fages map, again a tracing by a researcher who discovered it in the Archivo General de la Nación in Mexico City, was much clearer than the Goycoechea map and had some measurements that were omitted in the Goycoechea map (see figure 6).[8]

The Santa Barbara Presidio layout was approximately a rectangle, about 400 feet on each side, oriented on a northwest-southeast axis, with the entrance in the middle of the southeast side. The entrance gate was eleven feet wide. A walled passageway between the gate and the *plaza de armas*, or parade ground, provided access to two corrals, one on each side of the passageway. Each corral was 165 feet by 30 feet. With enough space to accommodate thirty to forty horses, they were conveniently located inside the defense wall. This arrangement permitted the soldiers to obtain their mounts in a hurry in case of an emergency and discouraged theft. The guardhouse, sheltering the soldier assigned to check those entering and leaving the presidio, was at the point where the passageway entered the parade ground. It connected to two small cells so that the guard could also watch prisoners.

The parade ground, approximately 325 feet square, was completely surrounded by buildings except at the entrances. Like modern-day cities subject to zoning, building uses were segregated to minimize friction between conflicting uses. Immediately to the right of, and convenient to, the entrance passageway were three large warehouses, each fifteen feet by fifty-five feet, in which were stored food and other supplies, equipment, clothing, etc. One contained the store where

---

[8]"Plan del Real Presidio del Canal de Santa Barbara," by Pedro Fages, September 16, 1788, MS in Map Collection of the Richman Papers, Newberry Library. Chicago, Illinois.

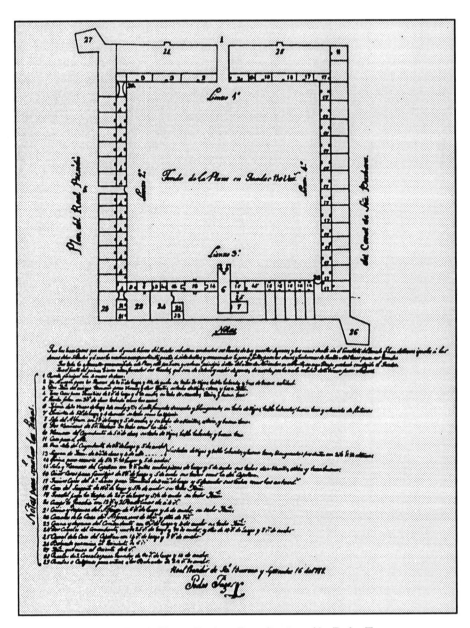

Figure 6: Plan of Santa Barbara Presidio signed by Pedro Fages.
Courtesy Richman Collection, Newberry Library.

supplies were sold to the soldiers and their families. To the left of the passageway, beyond the guardhouse and cells, were a barracks for single soldiers, quarters for the sergeants, and two rooms for soldiers' families.

Both sides of the parade ground were lined with family dwellings for the married soldiers. On the northeast side there were thirteen dwellings, each fourteen by twenty-two feet inside dimensions. On the southwest side there were thirteen, each fourteen by twenty-five feet in size. On the northeast side there was a "private gate" eight feet wide, the use of which was not given. It may have been intended as an escape route in case the main gate was blocked. It was roofed over in a possible attempt to make it look like the adjacent houses from the outside.

In the middle of the side of the parade ground opposite the main gate was the chapel, twenty-two feet by fifty-five feet, with a height of about twenty-one feet to the eave line. In addition to its religious function, the chapel in all probability served as a meeting place for the residents of the presidio and as a sanctuary for the women and children in case of attack. Its long axis was at right angles to the defense wall and to the adjacent buildings. It faced to the southeast. To the right of the chapel were the rooms reserved for the office and living quarters of the *comandante,* and next to those the living room and two bedrooms of the lieutenant. To the left of the chapel were two rooms for the chaplain and five family houses, probably for the families of the sergeants and corporals and for visitors.

Essentially, therefore, the working end of the presidio was on either side of the main gate, the administrative and religious side was opposite, and the family dwellings separated the two. Perhaps this design was intended to separate the squalling kids and barking dogs from the operations areas.

At the east and west corners were two bastions, shown on

the plan as diamond-shaped. A plan of the presidio drawn in pencil on heavy brown paper and generally in conformity with the Goycoechea plan is in the files of the Santa Barbara Mission Archive-Library.[9] A statement on this plan reads:

> The Santa Barbara Presidio was founded April 21, 1782, about twelve blocks southeast and two blocks southwest from the Mission on a spot where the present Canon Perdido and Santa Barbara Streets are crossing. Permanent buildings were commenced about 1785. The above plan is made after the description given to Mr. H. Bancroft, Hist. Cal. Vol. I, 464 and after measurements taken of the ruins by Mr. W. Hawley, 33, in 1895.

There is no signature. The plan shows the two bastions, but they are hexagonal. The diagram of the presidio shown on page 33 of Walter A. Hawley's book entitled *The Early Days of Santa Barbara, California,* shows only one bastion, at the east corner, and it is more or less round. The implication is that the bastion at the west corner of the presidio was never built, and to date its foundations have not been found.

In the preface to his book dated December 20, 1909, Hawley states:

> Fifteen years ago, realizing how rapidly the old landmarks were disappearing, the writer with the assistance of an engineer, made surveys both at the Mission and at the presidio of all the buildings then standing, and also of all the ruins and traces of foundations of former buildings. These surveys were then carefully platted.[10]

Conceivably the plan found in the Mission Archives is the plan prepared by Hawley.

Other than in books on military engineering relating to major forts in the Caribbean and in the Mediterranean area, or ones such as at St. Augustine, Florida, information on the design of the *revellines, baluartes* or bastions is meager; in fact, the difference between them is not entirely clear. *Webster's*

---

[9] Santa Barbara Mission Archive-Library, Map Collection.
[10] Hawley, *Early Days of Santa Barbara*, p. 3.

defines a bastion as a projecting part of a fortification.[11] It is the English term applied to the towers that extended outward from the defense wall surrounding a fort and designed to permit cannon to fire along the outside of each of the walls.

The dictionary of the Spanish language published by the Royal Spanish Academy defines a *revellín* as "an exterior structure that protects and defends the wall between two bastions of a fort." It defines a *baluarte* as "a structure of a fortification of pentagonal form that protrudes at the junction of two walls and is composed of two facades that form a salient angle, two flanks that join the walls and an entrance throat."

A drawing of the St. Augustine Presidio in Florida appearing as map 9 in the book *The Defenses of Spanish Florida* identifies the four diamond-shaped structures at the four corners as *baluartes* and a fifth entrance structure in the middle of one side, almost triangular in shape, as a *revellín*.[12]

In the Spanish documents describing the work of building the presidios and missions in California, the two words *revellín* and *baluarte* appear to be used almost interchangeably. However, it is concluded that a *revellín* is a simpler and less complex structure than a *baluarte*. If the definition appearing in the Royal Academy dictionary is being correctly interpreted, the word *revellín* should only be used to describe a structure between two bastions or *baluartes*. Since the California presidios and missions had only corner bastions, the designation of such a structure as a *revellín* is probably incorrect.

It is believed that the bastion or bastions of the Santa Barbara Presidio, if there were two, were projections at the corner of the presidio filled with earth to a height of about seven feet above the surrounding ground level. The cannon would

---

[11]Webster's *New Collegiate Dictionary*.

[12]Chatelain, *The Defenses of Spanish Florida*, map no. 9, following p. 192.

be mounted on top of the earth fill, hauled to that elevation by means of an earth ramp, and oriented to fire through crenelations in the top of the defense wall along an arc of some 270 degrees.

This conclusion is based upon a description of a bastion appearing in the annual report of the San Diego Mission for December 1778, which states that "a ravelin of adobe has been built, with double walls, an interior room with a flat roof, a stairway, and two doors with keys, one door above and the other below, to defend the east and north walls."[13]

The report for June 1783 prepared by Fr. Fermín Lasuén reads in part:

> There is a granary, twenty-five *varas* long and five and a half wide; a ravelin with high mezzanine with a pathway to ascend it, and with two doors...
>
> Taking all of these buildings into account, as well as the guard-house or quarters for the guards, they cover three sides of a square measuring fifty-five *varas*. As for the other side, a wall of adobe three *varas* [8¼ feet] high encloses it, and at one extremity it ends in a ravelin on the same floor but a little higher, and from this, and from the one already mentioned, it is possible for the four corners to be defended.[14]

It is concluded that some bastions were two-story affairs, with a ground floor room underneath the floor on which the cannon were emplaced. Other bastions apparently consisted of a raised floor of dirt fill which elevated the cannon so they could fire over the defense wall. The raised floor had a ramp from the surrounding ground level to enable the soldiers to move the cannon to that position. It would seem logical, considering the shortage of timbers to form the floor of the second story and strong enough to withstand the shock of the cannon discharge, together with the ease of filling the bas-

---

[13]Kenneally, *Writings of Lasuén*, II, 338.
[14]Kenneally, *Writings of Lasuén*, II, 364.

tion with dirt, that the dirt fill with ramp would have been the design used at Santa Barbara.

An important difference in the design of the Santa Barbara Presidio and many of those in the Southwest is that each of the Santa Barbara buildings surrounding the parade ground or plaza is provided with a back yard that backs up to the outer defense wall. Without this back yard, the defense wall formed the rear wall of the presidio buildings. The Santa Barbara design, therefore, called for a considerably larger quantity of adobe blocks to be made and laid for the separate walls.

The advantage of this design was creation of a private area for each dwelling in which could be located the latrines, woodpile, outdoor kitchen, domestic animals and even, perhaps, the cows, mules or horses owned by the occupant of the dwelling. The alternative was to have these accessory uses cluttering up the plaza. Animals could be brought through the dwelling from the plaza, since the dwelling floors were mostly dirt.

The rear yards were separated from each other by garden walls, probably three to five feet in height. The foundations of some of these walls have been uncovered in the course of archaeological excavations, and of course they show up on the 1788 plan.

It is conjectured that the back yards also served a defensive purpose. In the event attacking soldiers or Indians managed to surmount the outer defense wall, they would land in this back yard where they would be subject to fire from the back windows of the buildings. At the same time, they would be hemmed in by walls on four sides of their position, severely limiting their maneuverability. This, it would seem, was a major improvement over the former design that placed buildings abutting the outer defense wall, forcing the defending soldiers to crouch on top of the rear of the buildings behind the parapet of the defense wall, partially exposed to fire from beyond the wall. The logic of this conjecture has been questioned, and it must be admitted that there is no documentary proof nor was it ever tested by an attack. Whether or not the back yard design was planned as an added measure of defense, it appears that it would have made an attack less likely to be successful.

The original Monterey presidio as described by Fages in 1773 was built with the buildings abutting the outer defense wall.[15] After it was partially destroyed by fire in 1789, it was rebuilt following the back yard design.[16] As of 1792, however, the buildings on three sides of the San Francisco Presidio abutted the defense wall. The defense wall on the fourth side was almost nonexistent, and there were no bastions according to a report to then Governor José Antonio Roméu from Alférez Hermenegildo Sal, Habilitado and Acting Commandant at San Francisco.

One further detail of design was mentioned by Eugene Duflot de Mofras in his description of his travels in 1844.[17] He wrote:

> Presidios were invariably built in the following uniform manner: after a suitable place had been chosen, a trench about 4 meters [13 feet] broad and 2 [6.5 feet] deep was then excavated. What earth was removed was used for an outer embankment. The presidio was then enclosed by a quadrangle that measured approximately 200 meters [656 feet] on each side. The rampart, or wall, constructed of adobes, was 4 or 5 meters high and a meter thick [13 to 16 feet high and 3.3 feet thick], with small bastions at each corner. The presidio had only two gates...Within the presidio, the church, barracks for officers and soldiers, the houses of a few settlers, and the shops, stables, wells, and cisterns were provided.

As has already been mentioned, Ortega was directed to

---

[15]Horne, *A History of the Presidio of Monterey*, p. 11.
[16]Provincial State Papers, X, 167.
[17]Wilbur (trans. & ed.), *Duflot de Mofras' Travels*, vol. I, p. 142.

construct such a trench or dry moat before proceeding with any other construction at Santa Barbara, and there seems to be no good reason why, during the early period of the presidio, the moat would have been filled in. Fages's description of the Monterey presidio, mentioned above, states there were three trenches which commanded the front of the presidio.

No archaeological excavations have been undertaken to determine if the Santa Barbara Presidio had such a dry moat. In the mid-1970s a bottle buff started digging in the rear yard of the Bonilla House at 915 Santa Barbara Street. He found numerous old bottles in an area just outside the second defense wall. Earlier excavations in the rear of the Cañedo Adobe reportedly unearthed caches of old bottles. It is surmised that the original dry moat was used as a dump to get rid of bottles and other trash. If so, this could be a treasure trove of artifacts dating from the early 1800s to the 1840s and perhaps into the early 1900s.

Possible proof of the original existence of the dry moat at Santa Barbara appears in a corrected version of de Mofras's account of his travels. As translated from the French by Marguerite Eyer Wilbur, one paragraph reads: "The presidio, which was founded in 1780 [1782] is in ruins. Only a few sections of adobe walls are now standing; the jails, too, have crumbled, and the chapel alone has escaped destruction."[18] Since there was only one jail, the translation seemed suspect. Consultation with an expert in the French language, who translated from a copy of the original book published in French and available at the Santa Barbara Mission Archive-Library, produced the corrected sentence which reads: "The presidio, founded in 1780 [*sic*] is in ruins. Only a few sections of adobe walls remain standing; the ditches are filled and only

---

[18]Wilbur (trans. & ed.), *Duflot de Mofras' Travels*, I, 193-94.

the chapel is preserved."[19] Translations can be difficult, tricky and prone to certain errors. However, there is also the possibility that de Mofras assumed that all the presidios were surrounded by dry moats, and seeing none at Santa Barbara, assumed that it had been filled in. Still another possibility is that the ditch was excavated when the garrison first arrived at Santa Barbara as part of the palisade-type construction, but was filled in during construction of the permanent buildings. When archaeologists reach an area where such a trench might be located, the digging should be done in such a way that evidence could be uncovered.

A comparison of the design of the four Alta California presidios is easily made by reference to an article by this writer, entitled "Alta California's Four Fortresses," which reproduces all maps of the four presidios that have been discovered up to the date of its publication.[20] In each case, the presidio is a quadrangle, square or rectangular in shape, with a single main gate. A *plaza de armas*, or parade ground, is surrounded by presidio buildings, and the entire compound is surrounded by a defense wall, except at San Francisco, where the wall was unfinished. The separation of uses previously mentioned was more or less carried out at each presidio. Except at the first, San Diego, the church, padre's quarters and residences of the officers were opposite the main gate. At San Diego, the church was on the right side of the presidio facing the gate. The guardhouse, jail and storehouses were adjacent to the main gate in three of them. All except San Diego had back yards between the buildings and the defense wall. All were on high ground overlooking the anchorage and landing place.

---

[19] Duflot de Mofras, *Exploration de Territoire de L'Orégon, des Californies et de la Mer Vermille*, vol. I, p. 369.

[20] Whitehead, "Alta California's Four Fortresses," pp. 67-94.

Chronology of the Construction Period

Don Felipe de Goycoechea is credited with having supervised construction of all of the permanent buildings of the Santa Barbara Presidio. There is much that we do not know about him. In our research, his name first appears in a communication from Lt. José de Zúñiga, Commander of the San Diego Presidio, dated August 25, 1783, advising Governor Fages that Goycoechea had arrived at San Diego the previous day and was leaving the next day with five troopers for their destination.[1] Just how and where he spent his time during the next four months has not been discovered. He was not listed on the manpower report of the Santa Barbara Presidio for December 2, 1783, but a communication dated February 10, 1784, from the governor to his commanding general states that the command of the Santa Barbara Presidio passed from Ortega to Goycoechea on the previous January 25th. The company then consisted of Goycoechea, Alférez José Argüello, three sergeants, two corporals, and fifty privates, a total of fifty seven men, of whom fifteen were stationed at San Buenaventura Mission.

When Goycoechea assumed command, the palisade presidio had been completed, water from Mission Creek flowed to the front gate of the presidio, and the soldiers had sown

---

[1]Provincial State Papers, III, 412.

seventeen *fanegas* (about thirty acres) of wheat, presumably in the vicinity of the ditch from Mission Creek west of the presidio. One note states they planned to harvest the wheat early in July 1784, so the presidio was at least partially self-supporting by that time. At Los Angeles, where the settlers were supposed to produce crops for the presidios, they had planted fifty-six acres of wheat, plus beans and other crops.

Reports on the progress of construction gleaned from the documents pertaining to this period will be given in chronological order. Unless quotation marks are used to indicate a verbatim account, the entries represent a translation of a report summarized from a document by one of Bancroft's scribes.

JUNE 30, 1784. Goycoechea to Governor Fages. On the 14th of this month the first adobes were begun for the construction of the three storehouses, guardhouse, barracks, and three houses contained in the first facade of buildings. Don Esteban Martínez, captain of the frigate *Favorita*, has offered to make his crew available for work on the presidio when he arrives in Santa Barbara. It would be very helpful if arrangements could be made for six sailors to remain in Santa Barbara to make adobes, for the garrison alone is not enough.[2]

> COMMENTARY. As will be pointed out later, archaeological excavations in 1974 uncovered the cornerstone in the south corner of the presidio defense wall. This, plus the designation of *Lienzo* 1 (first stretch of wall, or side number one) on the Goycoechea and Fages maps, plus the sequence of building construction, proves that the southeast side of the quadrangle, closest to De la Guerra Street and containing the main entrance gate, was the first to be constructed. Top priority was given to construction of this side because it contained the storehouse for food, clothing and other supplies. These materials could be severely damaged if exposed to sun, wind and

[2]Provincial State Papers, IV, 477-78.

rain. Three storehouses or warehouses were located in the first facade.

JULY 1, 1784. Goycoechea submits to Fages a *padrón*, or census, of the members of the Santa Barbara company, stating whether they are present or absent, and if absent, where. There are sixty officers and men with one soldier's position vacant. A summary shows the following:[3]

On guard in the presidio	10
Guarding the horses	5
On duty in San Buenaventura	15
Watchman for the town of Los Angeles	1
On the frontier of the Californias	1
With the mail service to San Diego	4
Cutting timber in Monterey	1
With the mule train to the town of Los Angeles	5
Available for duty	18
Total	60

AUGUST 1784. Governor Fages to José Cañizares, captain of the packetboat *San Carlos*. Convicts are cutting timber for the Santa Barbara Presidio [presumably at Monterey].[4]

AUGUST 4, 1784. Governor Fages requests Viceroy Matías de Gálvez to authorize assignment of six to eight sailors from the next supply ship to be left at Santa Barbara to help in construction since they have only eighteen soldiers available to work.[5]

COMMENTARY. The request was denied at first, but later it was approved.

AUGUST 8, 1784. Goycoechea to Governor Fages. The work on the presidio is progressing at an extraordinary pace.[6]

---

[3]*Archivo General de la Nación, Obras Públicas, tomo* 15.
[4]Provincial Record, II, 313.   [5]Provincial Record, II, 309.
[6]Provincial State Papers, IV, 470-71.

DECEMBER 23, 1784. Goycoechea acknowledges information that Private Eugenio Rosalio, a stonemason, and Manuel Rodríguez, a carpenter, are to report to his company.[7]

DECEMBER 31, 1784. Manpower Report shows:

On Guard duty at the Presidio	10
Guarding the horses at the Presidio	5
Detached to Mission San Buenaventura	15
On escort duty	1
On guard duty at Los Angeles	1
Courier with the mail	4
With the pack train for provisions	5
On the frontier of the Californias	1
Available for duty	18
Total	60[8]

MARCH 9, 1785. Joseph Antonio Rengel, who has replaced Teodoro de Croix as Commanding General of the Internal Provinces and now has headquarters in Chihuahua, orders Fages to found the Mission of Santa Barbara in Montecito and reports that the *Audiencia Gobernadora* of Mexico has authorized the usual 1,000 pesos for the founding of a mission.[9]

JUNE 28, 1785. Goycoechea reports to Governor Fages insubordination by Private Rosalio, the stonemason sent to work on the presidio. When ordered in front of some Indians to do certain work, he refused and replied uncivilly. Upon being ordered to come down off a wall, the soldier refused and defended himself with a pick, whereupon Goycoechea mounted the wall, pushed him off the wall and placed him in confinement.[10]

[7]Provincial State Papers, IV, 470.
[8]Junípero Serra Collection, No. 1005a, in Santa Barbara Mission Archive-Library.
[9]California Mission Documents, No. 9, in Santa Barbara Mission Archive-Library.
[10]Provincial State Papers, V, 158.

AUGUST 9, 1785. Goycoechea reports to Governor Fages that he is experimenting with the use of twenty to thirty Indians as workers on the construction of the presidio because of the scarcity of supplies. Cultivating the ground for planting will begin. They are completing fabrication of the tiles for roofing the three warehouses and, rains permitting, a start will be made on the guardhouse and barracks.[11]

AUGUST 25, 1785. Goycoechea informs Governor Fages that approval has been given to the transfer of eight sailors from the packetboat *Aránzazu* for work at the Santa Barbara Presidio.[12]

SEPTEMBER 13, 1785. Governor Fages informs Goycoechea that he is sending sixty beams from Monterey to Santa Barbara.[13]

OCTOBER 7, 1785. Goycoechea reports to Governor Fages arrival of the frigate *Favorita* with sixty beams and thirty-two *fanegas* of corn. Requests return of the shackles worn by Eugenio Rosalio, the stonemason sent to work on the presidio.[14]

COMMENTARY. It is conjectured that the sixty beams were for the three warehouses. As will later be noted, the 1788 description of the presidio by Goycoechea and Fages states that there was one storehouse for supplies, twenty *varas* in length and five and a half in width, its roof of *vigas* (beams), *tablas labradas* (finished boards), and good quality tile. This statement has been interpreted to mean that the beams spanned the width of the building and that on top of the beams was placed smooth planking, creating a loft where goods could be stored. Two other storehouses had the same dimensions and were for provisions and other effects, with a roof of beams, *estibas* (wattles) and tile. The wattles are interpreted to be reeds placed on top of rafters. The total length of the three buildings was 165 feet. The 1788 description differentiates between rafters (*mar-*

---

[11]Provincial State Papers, V, 156-57.
[12]Provincial State Papers, V, 176.
[13]Provincial State Papers, V, 223.
[14]Provincial State Papers, V, 167.

rillos), used in the family rooms, and beams, used in the storehouses and church. This nomenclature will be discussed in more detail in another chapter.

OCTOBER 25, 1785. Goycoechea to Governor Fages. Sends names of eight seamen who are working on the construction of the presidio. The three warehouses are roofed with tile and he will see if he can do the guardhouse with a roof of mortar as an experiment, since he intends to continue the work if obstacles do not prevent it.[15]

DECEMBER 12, 1785. Goycoechea reports to Governor Fages that a Gentile (unconverted Indian) hit a priest with a stick, for which reason he was made a prisoner in shackles. It is necessary to finish the warehouses and guard room.[16]

DECEMBER 31, 1785. Goycoechea submits to Governor Fages a *padrón*, or census, of the population of Santa Barbara. It lists by name fifty-five officers and men of the garrison, their race, their ages, whether married or single and if married, the names, ages and race of their wives and the number and ages of their children.[17]

JANUARY 20, 1786. Goycoechea reports to Governor Fages that he has carried out the governor's orders that the gentiles not be permitted to enter the presidio. The curiosity of these natives is wellknown, especially upon the arrival of the governor or *padres* (priests).[18]

FEBRUARY 17, 1786. Goycoechea reports to Governor Fages that the horses are pastured on the far side of Mescaltitán (Goleta) and are guarded by nine men and one corporal. Commentary on number of men arriving for construction. They are working on the foundations and transporting stone.[19]

[15]Provincial State Papers, V, 168.
[17]State Papers, Missions, I, 5-10.
[19]Provincial State Papers, VI, 301.
[16]Provincial State Papers, V, 172-73.
[18]Provincial State Papers, VI, 322-23.

MARCH 20, 1786. Goycoechea reports to Governor Fages that the rains are impeding progress of the work on the buildings, the stone is being carried in and, this week, wood will be cut for the roofs.[20]

MAY 28, 1786. Goycoechea writes to Governor Fages requesting a carpenter who is needed to construct the granaries, the lack of which has caused the loss of some corn. He has had 20,000 adobe bricks made which they will start laying June 1. Twelve San Gabriel Indians are working on the presidio.[21]

JUNE 8, 1786. Goycoechea reports to Governor Fages that on the first of this month they began to erect walls for the soldiers' barracks and sergeant's quarters. He requested a carpenter for construction of the granaries.[22]

JULY 19, 1786. Goycoechea reports to Governor Fages that the wheat harvest is finished, that they are making adobes for erecting the walls of the second facade and will begin the roofs.[23]

JULY 25, 1786. Goycoechea reports to Governor Fages that the plantings of corn at Los Angeles have contracted rust. He plans to start on the masonry work at the presidio and complains of the lack of water, timber and roof tiles.[24]

SEPTEMBER 29, 1786. Goycoechea reports to Governor Fages the arrival in the harbor of the frigate *Favorita*. The wheat harvest at Los Angeles amounts to more than 500 bushels and at the presidio, 170 bushels. They have covered the guardhouse, sergeant's quarters and five soldiers' houses with tile, and 5000 tiles are left to be baked. He hopes to finish by the middle of October the two sides of the quadrangles

---

[20]Provincial State Papers, VI, 319.   [21]Provincial State Papers, VI, 318-19.
[22]Provincial State Papers, VI, 306.   [23]Provincial State Papers, VI, 328.
[24]Provincial State Papers, VI, 330.

into which he will move the troops who are in danger in their dwellings.[25]

> COMMENTARY. The danger apparently refers to the possibility that the palisade buildings constructed to house the soldiers and their families are now almost two and a half years old, have survived two winters' storms, and are in danger of collapse.

OCTOBER 21, 1786. Goycoechea reports to Governor Fages that the frigate *Princesa* anchored at Santa Barbara on the 19th and delivered 58 *morrillos* (short timbers) and 12 beams sent by the governor. At first they were able to put on shore in a barge only 40 *morrillos* and 5 *vigas gruesas* (large beams) with the help of Captain Martínez. The Captain will help make some adobes and, if time permits, assist in construction of the houses of the officers. The roofs of the houses are already covered with roof tile.[26]

NOVEMBER 13, 1786. Goycoechea reports to Governor Fages that palings have been cut and dragged to the site of the new Mission Santa Barbara. They are preparing to sow in the vicinity of the presidio. The families have moved into their new dwellings. Scarcely had that occurred when all of the facade of the old guardhouse and warehouses came down without a mishap. This necessitated putting two families in each dwelling, and now it is necessary to close the quadrangle and demolish everything that is old and may fall.[27]

NOVEMBER 28, 1786. A baptism was performed in the Commander's quarters because the [palisade] presidio chapel threatened to collapse.[28] According to the presidio baptismal register, the baptized child was named Joseph Basilio Lobo. The father was the presidio soldier Juan Joseph Lobo, native

---

[25]Provincial State Papers, VI, 313.

[26]Provincial State Papers, VI, 307-08.

[27]Provincial State Papers, VI, 316-17.

[28]Entry No. 32 in Santa Barbara Baptismal Register, November 28, 1786, in Santa Barbara Mission Archive-Library.

of the Villa de Sinaloa, and the mother was María Nicolasa Beltrán, native of the Presidio of San Miguel de Horcasitas in Sonora.

DECEMBER 3, 1786. According to the presidio marriage register, the first marriage solemnized at the presidio was performed in the building used as the guardhouse because the [palisade] presidio chapel threatened to collapse.[29] Joseph Calisto, son of Nicolás de Ayala and Alegría Ygnacio, natives of Real de Cosalá, was married to Juana Vitala Feliz, daughter of Vitoreno and María Michaela Landena, natives of the same city.

DECEMBER 5, 1786. Goycoechea to Fages. The families are lodged in the new buildings and the quadrangle is now enclosed with a stockade.[30]

JANUARY 21, 1787. According to the presidio death register, a child named Joseph Antonio Domínguez, son of Joseph María Domínguez, a presidio soldier, and María Marcelina Vidal, was buried in front of the presidio chapel because the [palisade] chapel threatened to collapse.[31]

FEBRUARY 3, 1787. Goycoechea to Fages. The people are riprapping (filling up the chinks of the wall with small stones and mortar) the existing walls with mortar in order to prevent the rain from eroding the adobe.[32]

JUNE 12, 1787. The first marriage of a presidio soldier at the newly-constructed Santa Barbara Mission was performed, a practice continued by many soldiers, although many were also married in the presidio chapel. According to the marriage register, Hilario Giménez, a native of Tepic and

---

[29]Entry No. 1 in Santa Barbara Mission Marriage Register, December 3, 1786, in Santa Barbara Mission Archive-Library.

[30]Provincial State Papers, VI, 321.

[31]Entry No. 9 in Santa Barbara Presidio Burial Register, January 21, 1787, in Santa Barbara Mission Archive-Library.

[32]Provincial State Papers, VII, 66.

a member of the Santa Barbara Mission guard, was married to an Indian neophyte of the *ranchería* of *Siugtú* named Juana María.[33]

JUNE 24, 1787. Goycoechea reports to Governor Fages that the muddy condition of the ground does not permit the movement of the ox-carts to carry stones, and for that reason, consideration is being given to start the cutting of wood in the wane of the moon, unless another rainy spell prevents it. By this time the front wall will be covered with mortar for better preservation and security.[34]

JULY 31, 1787. First burial in the new presidio chapel. It was a two-year-old infant named Inocencio Joseph Rodríguez, son of Joseph Manuel Rodríguez, native of Guadalupe, Mexico, and of María Valenzuela, native of Villa de Sinaloa.[35]

COMMENTARY. In view of the entry for November 3, 1787, it can be assumed that the permanent presidio chapel of adobe was completed and consecrated by this date. Since the chapel was lengthened in 1797, this burial and any others prior to December 1797 may have been located closer to the chapel entrance rather than in front of the steps to the altar of the lengthened chapel. From November 1787 to 1789, burials of presidio soldiers and members of their families occurred in the presidio chapel. After 1789, many burials occurred in the Santa Barbara Mission cemetery.

NOVEMBER 3, 1787. Goycoechea submits to Governor Fages a census and manpower and building status reports for the presidio. Manpower is one lieutenant, three sergeants, two corporals and fifty privates. There are 124 horses and 109 mules. The third facade of the presidio is completed with the church, houses of the officers, chaplain's quarters and five soldiers' quarters.[36]

---

[33]Entry No. 3 in Santa Barbara Presidio Marriage Register, June 12, 1787, in Santa Barbara Mission Archive-Library.   [34]Provincial State Papers, VII, 60.
[35]Entry No. 10, Santa Barbara Presidio Burial Register, July 31, 1787, in Santa Barbara Mission Archive-Library.   [36]State Papers, Sacramento, I, 5-8.

NOVEMBER 10, 1787. Goycoechea reports to Fages that he wishes to cover the walls before the rains come.[37]

APRIL 2, 1788. Francisco Hijosa, *Comisario* of the San Blas Supply Depot, reports to Viceroy Manuel Flores that he has been informed by naval personnel who visited the Santa Barbara Presidio last October 3rd, that two sides of the quadrangle had been completed, the third side had been started, and the fourth side had been laid out. Its circumference was some 400 or more *varas* within which square was the church. The dwellings of those who live there were ready. The captain of the presidio intends to build at the rear of the defense wall a corral and kitchen of adobe.[38]

AUGUST 1, 1788. Governor Fages reports to Viceroy Flores that when he was at Santa Barbara last, he found that they had finished three sides of the quadrangle. In the first side, they had three storehouses, a guard room, barracks and three houses; in the second, fourteen houses and a small barracks; and in the third, two houses for the commander and his lieutenant, the church, the house for the chaplain and five houses for families of the troops. The walls are of double adobe (blocks) on foundations of stone. The roofs are of wood and tile of good quality which is made there, and the casemate roof is the same. Currently, they are raising the walls of fifteen houses (in the fourth side of the quadrangle) so that in this year the inside square will be enclosed. The plaza (parade ground) has a net dimension of 133 *varas* (366 feet). In the following year and some part of the one after that, they will finish the defense wall with its bastions.[39]

COMMENTARY. This is the first and, so far, the only reference to a casemate, the structure for housing powder and ammunition for

---

[37]Provincial State Papers, VII, 72.

[38]*Archivo General de la Nación, Obras Públicas, tomo* 15, No. 34, dated April 2, 1788.

[39]*Archivo General de la Nación, Obras Públicas, tomo* 15, Nos. 110 and 112, dated August 1, 1788.

the troops. It is believed to be located close to the bastion at the east corner of the presidio. On the basis of a sketch of the layout of the presidio by F. L. Birabent, an early owner of the Rochin Adobe at 820 Santa Barbara Street, which shows a "vault" in the rear yard of that adobe, the casement is believed to be on that property.

On September 23, 1788, Fages corrected the dimensions of the plaza to 110 *varas* (302.5 feet) instead of 133 *varas*.

AUGUST 23, 1788. The Indian Burial Register of Mission Santa Barbara records the burial of the Indian Joseph Cayetano, about eighteen years old, who died when he fell into a well at the presidio while cleaning it out.[40]

COMMENTARY. This is the earliest record of a well being located within the presidio quadrangle. Its location is, so far, unknown, but when found, it should yield many early artifacts.

SEPTEMBER 16, 1788. Commanding Officer Goycoechea prepared and signed a drawing of the presidio with a statement of the status of building construction as of that date, plus a brief description of each structure, giving the dimensions of rooms, details of the roofs, floors and walls and the use of each room. The original apparently was destroyed in the San Francisco fire of 1906, but as earlier indicated, Bancroft had his scribes copy it on tracing cloth, using both sides.[41] The document was forwarded to Fages who had another copy prepared, a copy upon which there are a few measurements that do not appear on the Goycoechea copy. This permitted clearing up a discrepancy of about forty feet between measurements on the map and the measurements taken on the ground between the northeasterly and southwesterly sides of the parade ground after the foundations were uncovered by archaeological excavations and plotted on a map.

OCTOBER 21, 1788. Goycoechea reports to Governor Fages

---

[40]Entry No. 17 in Santa Barbara Mission Indian Burial Register, dated August 23, 1788 in Santa Barbara Mission Archive-Library.

[41]Provincial State Papers, XII, 61.

Figure 7: Watercolor painting of Santa Barbara Presidio
Chapel by Navy Lt. James Alden, 1855. Courtesy Santa
Barbara Mission Archive-Library.

Fages that the quadrangle is closed and the roofs of tile finished, *Puntales* have been put in place provisionally in the
houses.[42]

COMMENTARY. The word *puntal* is translated in various dictionar-
ies as a stanchion, stay, support or pillar. Usually the definition
states that it is used to support a wall that threatens to collapse. It is
not clear how such a support would be used, since all the buildings
on this date were new and there should have been no threat of collapse. Possibly this word is used to define posts upholding the
porch which is believed to have been in place along the fronts of all
the buildings, as is depicted in an 1855 Alden painting of the presidio chapel on the building north of the chapel (see figure 7).[43] No
written proof of the existence of the porch, or *corredor*, has been
found, and this is one item to be remembered as archaeological
excavations proceed.[44]

---

[42]Provincial State Papers, VII, 298-99.

[43]Naval Lt. James Alden was a U.S. Coast Survey cartographer who painted many water
colors of early California scenes in the mid-1800s. *Ed. note.*

[44]Archaeological investigations of the Presidio's northeast corner through 1994 have
uncovered a drip line which indicates that there was no covered porch along this portion of
the quadrangle. *Ed. note.*

NOVEMBER 22, 1788. Goycoechea thanks Governor Fages for having praised the excellence of the presidio construction and says he will do his best on what remains to be done on the project.[45]

NOVEMBER 22, 1788. Goycoechea acknowledges to Governor Fages receipt of the beams which Captain Martínez delivered in the *Princesa*. He has not been able to use them because of the rainy season, but the houses are secured with *puntales*.[46]

> COMMENTARY. This would imply that *puntales* were used as stanchions or bracing to support the walls, perhaps those that were freestanding and were not supported by right-angled integrated walls.

DECEMBER 31, 1788. Goycoechea's year-end report to Fages on the manpower at his garrison shows the following:[47]

Assignments	Lt.	Ens.	Sgts.	Corps.	Priv.	Total
Presidio Guard					5	5
Guard for the Horse Herd					4	4
Detachment at San Buenaventura		1			10	11
Detachment at Santa Barbara Mission			1		2	3
Detachment at Purísima Mission			1		14	15
Detachment at San Gabriel Mission					1	1
Detachment at San Diego Presidio					3	3
Detachment at Loreto Presidio					1	1
Mail couriers to Monterey					3	3
Available for service	1	1	1	__	10	13
Totals	1	1	2	2	53	59

---

[45]Provincial State Papers, VII, 275.   [46]Provincial State Papers, VII, 285.
[47]Provincial State Papers, VII, 273.

JUNE 26, 1789. Goycoechea reports to Governor Fages that he has finished two sides of the defense wall with about a half *vara* (about 1½ feet) of stone, the third side is in progress and as soon as they are finished, the ox-carts will be unloaded in order to begin erection of the defense wall (with adobe bricks).[48]

AUGUST 27, 1789. Goycoechea reports to Governor Fages that the defense wall now measures 2½ *varas* (about 7 feet) in height on the chapel side and half a *vara* (about 1½ feet) on the other two sides. Although he does not have an expert (stonemason or artisan), he hopes to finish the three sides of the defense wall which obviously seems desirable, and when finished, to order acquisition of the lime for mortar (presumably for plastering the sides of the defense wall).[49]

SEPTEMBER 19, 1789. Goycoechea reports to Governor Fages that half the defense wall is finished, with a height of three and a half *varas* (9.6 feet), and he is going to lay down the floor of *ladrillos* (floor tiles) and mortar. He has some 5000 tiles ready to fire, and some mortar.[50]

COMMENTARY. It is conjectured that the floor tiles were for the chapel.

APRIL 29, 1790. Alférez Pablo Cota reports to Governor Fages that the mule train continues to haul grain from Los Angeles where it has been harvested but badly stored. The work continues, carrying stones for the foundations and reinforcing the roads as time permits. The wheat crop does not look promising up to now.[51]

COMMENTARY. It is possible that this report and the next one pertain to work at La Purísima Mission, although the document is marked from Santa Barbara. Cota was earlier stationed at La Purísima.

---

[48]Provincial State Papers, IX, 110.
[49]Provincial State Papers, IX, 85.
[50]Provincial State Papers, IX, 99.
[51]Provincial State Papers, IX, 150.

APRIL 29, 1790. Cota reports to Fages. With Juan María Pinto goes Juan Mejías, and they carry nine new spades or mattocks, three picks and a crowbar, since although two remain here, one is broken and the other lacks a point. I find myself with the necessity of having to shape stone for the foundations of the walls, and without the ability to repair it.[52]

JULY 6, 1790. Goycoechea reports to Fages that he has given to the Viceroy an account of the state of construction of the presidio. The foundations of the wall that is lacking have been set up. This report has not been found.[53]

JULY 6, 1790. Goycoechea reports to Governor Fages that he has assembled the members of the company and has asked them if they will contribute (help pay the payments) to those (Indians) who are working on the construction of the presidio, and they have agreed to it. Goycoechea also reports he has decided to finish the two sides of the defense wall that are incomplete, and to remove the roof of the chapel in order to repair it since the walls are much exposed.[54]

> COMMENTARY. It is conjectured from the above statement that the original roof of the chapel may have been constructed without a sufficient overhang to the eaves, thus exposing the walls to erosion from rain.

AUGUST 21, 1790. Goycoechea submits a report to Governor Fages listing the names of the officers, soldiers and other residents of the presidio; their race, age and place of birth; the name, race and age of their wives; and the names and ages of their children. There are sixty-one officers and soldiers and six other men listed. With their wives and children, there were 230 people living in the presidio.[55]

Statistics were as follows:[56]

---

[52]Provincial State Papers, IX, 148.   [53]Provincial State Papers, IX, 169.
[54]Provincial State Papers, IX, 170.
[55]Provincial State Papers, Benicia Military, XIII, 448-54.
[56]State Papers, Missions, I, 96.

Men: Single 82, married 44, widowers 5.

Women: Single 55, married 43, widows 1.

Europeans 2, Spaniards 124, *Mestizos* 52, Indians 17, Mulattos 35.

Men with the military force 61, tailors 2, laborers 2.

COMMENTARY. *Mestizos*, also called *Coyotes*, are individuals having a Spanish father and an Indian mother. Indians listed here are not necessarily of the local Chumash tribe, since some Indians were brought up from Mexico both as recruits and as interpreters and servants.

SEPTEMBER 10, 1790. Governor Fages sends a memorandum to the Viceroy listing the artisans needed at each of the four presidios for servicing the presidios and training the natives at the missions. For the Santa Barbara Presidio, he lists the need for two carpenters, two iron workers, one armorer, two masons and a weaver, a foreman, a tanner, a stone-cutter, a tailor and a potter.[57]

FEBRUARY 26, 1791. Governor Fages writes a memorandum to Lt. Col. José Antonio Roméu, who is succeeding him as governor. In it he reviews the status of the various presidios. For Santa Barbara, he states that the construction is finished except for a short section (probably of the defense wall) which will be finished this year.[58]

APRIL 7, 1792. Viceroy Revilla Gigedo sends to Governor Roméu a plan for construction of the Monterey presidio chapel approved by the Director of Architecture of the Academy of San Carlos in Mexico City, the organization designated to design and approve such structures. This organization was not created until 1779, which may account for the fact that no plan for the Santa Barbara Chapel has so far been found.[59]

---

[57]State Papers, Missions, I, 84.

[58]Provincial State Papers, X, 152-69.

[59]State Papers, Sacramento, I, 113.

DECEMBER 30, 1792. Goycoechea submits to the governor a listing of all the individuals who contributed to the payment of Indians who worked on the construction of the presidio between 1786 and 1789, including the amounts contributed. The list includes the dates during this period when eighteen soldiers were discharged, presumably because their ten-year enlistment period was up. Four soldiers died during this period and one was transferred to another unit.[60]

DECEMBER 31, 1792. Goycoechea submits to the governor a report on the census and races at the Santa Barbara Presidio, as follows:[61]

Males: Unmarried 94, Married 49, Widowers 4.
Females: Unmarried 53, Married 49.
Spanish 144, *Mestizos* 46, Indians 10, Mulattos 47.
Men with the military force 63, Tailors 2, Laborers 3,
   Muleteers 4.

AUGUST 20, 1793. Governor José Joaquín de Arrillaga reports to Viceroy Revilla Gigedo on the status of all the presidios. For Santa Barbara, he states that although it was begun last, it is the most complete owing to the activity of its commander. It lacks only the repair of some of the roofs of the houses that were made of poor wood. All will be finished by the coming year except the chapel, which needs to be lengthened somewhat, and construction of a cemetery outside of the quadrangle.[62]

NOVEMBER 10-18, 1793. English Captain George Vancouver visited at Santa Barbara with his three ships, the *Discovery*, the *Chatham*, and the *Daedalus*.[63] Vancouver describes the oil slick on the surface of the sea, probably in the vicinity

[60]Provincial State Papers, XII, 62.
[61]State Papers, Missions, I, 103.
[62]Provincial State Papers, XXI, 115.
[63]"Menzies' California Journal of the Vancouver Expedition," p. 320; and Wilbur (ed.), *Vancouver in California*, vol. II, p. 150.

of Coal Oil Point, as covered with a thick slimy substance which, when agitated, became very luminous and smelled like burning tar or some such resinous substance. (Oil slicks in this area have more recently been attributed to the oil platforms and to tanker operations). Of Santa Barbara, he comments that it bore the appearance of a far more civilized place than any other of the Spanish settlements:

> The buildings appeared to be regular and well constructed, the walls clean and white, and the roofs of the houses were covered with a bright red tile. The presidio was the nearest to the sea shore, and just showed itself above a grove of small trees, producing with the rest of the buildings a very picturesque effect.

Vancouver visited with Goycoechea at the presidio, which Vancouver described as forming a large square space surrounded by a range of barracks and storehouses situated on a delightful plain backed by a hilly ridge. Goycoechea loaned Vancouver a *carreta* (two-wheel cart) drawn by oxen to gather wood and water to replenish the ships' supplies. Brackish water was obtained from a source close to the beach used by other visiting Spanish ships, but Vancouver's men found a much finer source close by. However, they obtained part of their supply from "a large well of excellent water" located within the presidio walls.

The English visitor expressed surprise that in this remote corner of the globe, most of the plates and dishes on which dinner at the presidio was served were of English manufactory, and "though they were but common stoneware, yet the commandant placed great value on them and assured us he was proud in being possessed of them." Vancouver said that the presidio excels all the others in neatness, cleanliness and other smaller though essential comforts and that it is placed on an elevated part of the plain and is raised some feet from the ground by a basement story which adds much to its pleasantness.

COMMENTARY. Reference to the basement story is an enigma, since of course there was none. Possibly because the northwest side of the quadrangle in which the commandant's quarters were located is about eight feet above the southeast side because of the two percent slope of the land, Vancouver probably thought the difference in elevation was due to a basement story.

MAY 7, 1794. A communication from Governor Arrillaga to Hermenegildo Sal, Commandant at the San Francisco Presidio, includes information that the Indians at Santa Barbara working on the presidio are paid at the rate of one and a half *reales* a day and an *almud* [about five quarts] of corn.[64]

OCTOBER 11, 1794. Goycoechea reports that in order to conclude all the works of the Santa Barbara Presidio, he must have the work of fifteen day-laborers [presumably Indians] for six months at one and a half *reales* per day each and thirty-four *fanegas* of corn.[65]

OCTOBER 17, 1794. In compliance with an order from the Viceroy, the Marqués de Branciforte, Engineer Miguel Costansó prepared a report on a plan for strengthening the presidios of New California. The Viceroy was aware of the vulnerability of the California coast to invasion by foreign powers, and particularly so in view of the renewed activity of Russia and England in the Pacific.[66]

COMMENTARY. Costansó did not visit the various ports and presidios of California at this time, although he was familiar with the coastline, having participated in the expedition of 1769 under Governor Portolá which traveled from San Diego to San Francisco Bay. He relied upon information furnished him by the Viceroy. His conclusion was that Spain could not afford the tremendous expense of so fortifying the 500-mile coastline as to make it impregnable to invasion. Instead, he recommended an accelerated program of settlement to build up the population of subjects of the King of Spain,

[64]Provincial Record, II, 364-65.
[65]Provincial State Papers, XII, 63.
[66]Servín (trans), "Costansó's 1794 Report."

supplemented by encouragement of coastwise shipping for fishing and trade.

OCTOBER 24, 1794. Regulations were issued, presumably by Goycoechea, that included a warning that construction expenses should be stopped, that only expenses absolutely indispensable to conclude the work of the presidio chapel and maintain what stands would be allowed.[67]

DECEMBER 13, 1794. Governor Diego de Borica writes to Goycoechea stating that on a recent trip to the Santa Barbara Presidio, the troops of the garrison agreed to make the small repairs to their respective corrals themselves. Also since the cost of lengthening the chapel is very small and will be paid out of the Gratuity Fund, the 1200 *pesos* designated for that purpose is to be distributed among the troops in accord with a schedule which he incorporates in the letter.[68]

APRIL 27, 1795. Governor Borica orders Goycoechea to continue work on the wall whenever possible.[69]

JUNE 17-20, 1795. Sergeant Felipe María Ortega writes a diary on a trip to the Santa Ynez Valley to reconnoiter locations for a mission to the north of Santa Barbara. He and three soldiers left the presidio at 8 A.M. and arrived at the Zanja de Cota (now the town of Santa Ynez) at 5 P.M. Continuing northward the next day, he found a large grove of pines, easy to take out since they had procured some previously for the presidio. He found eight *rancherías* in the vicinity. The Indians were friendly. On the 19th, he traveled by way of what is now Refugio Pass to the *ranchería* of Dos Pueblos, and the next day returned to the presidio.[70]

COMMENTARY. The grove of pines was just east of where the

---

[67]Provincial State Papers, XII, 98-99.
[68]Provincial State Papers, XII, 59-60.
[69]Provincial Record, IV, 291-92.
[70]Provincial State Papers, XII, 242-44.

Figueroa Mountain Road crosses Alamo Pintado Creek and starts up the grade to Figueroa Mountain.

JULY 23, 1795. Governor Borica writes Goycoechea that since there is no wood at San Diego from which to make *carretas* in which to carry materials to build the *castillo* (battery) of Fort Guijarros, it is easiest to transport it from Santa Barbara by the supply ship. Therefore Goycoechea should order immediately the cutting of twenty round trunks of oak, stripped and carried to the beach.[71]

> COMMENTARY. The Viceroy had ordered the construction of *castillos*, or outlying batteries of cannon, at San Francisco, Monterey and San Diego. At San Francisco, the battery was at Fort Point at the southerly end of what is now the Golden Gate Bridge. It was called the Battery of San Joaquín. At Monterey, it was located on what is now called the Presidio. At San Diego, it was located on what is now called Ballast Point, nearly out to the end of Point Loma. The *castillo* at Santa Barbara was not built until the 1830s.

AUGUST 27, 1795. Governor Borica orders Goycoechea to have lumber cut for twenty oxen yokes to be shipped on the frigate *Aránzazu*.[72]

SEPTEMBER 14, 1795. Goycoechea reports to Governor Borica that the twenty wheel hubs, forty fellies (wheel rims), ten axles and twenty yokes which were ordered for the presidio of San Diego will be ready.[73]

> COMMENTARY. Wheel hubs, axles, fellies and yokes for oxen had to be made of very strong wood such as oak. It seems strange that Santa Barbara could be a source for exporting wood, but it was the only port where oak trees grew close to the beach and the wood could easily be hauled to the ship.

MARCH 12, 1796. Goycoechea forwards to Governor Borica a list of nineteen villages of Gentiles along the coast between San Buenaventura and Point Pedernales, as follows:

---

[71]Provincial Record, IV, 295.   [72]Provincial Record, IV, 295.
[73]Provincial State Papers, XIV, 67.

Village and population	Chief	Distance between villages
Sisolopo (San Buenaventura), 86	Linguiguiy	
El Rincón, 68	None	5 leagues
La Carpintería, 97	Pachafaguay	1
El Paredón, 31	Atasuit	1
El Montecito, 62	Sagapueje (woman)	1
Yuctu (Santa Barbara), 125	Yanonali	1
Sacpili (Goleta), 202	Yununachet	2
Alcas (Goleta), 51	Sumumaquil	
Gelijec (Goleta), 66	Aquiait	
Geló (Goleta), 101	Guiguiahuit	
Miquiqui (Dos Pueblos), 210	Yguamaitu	3
Casil (Refugio), 142	Tenuaguichet	
	Siesanapaciet	3
La Quemada, 250	Snigulaisu	1
La Gaviota, 99	Asiquiyaut	3
El Bulito, 68	Tulul	2
Santa Texas, 30	Suluguapuyaut	2
Sisilopo, 72	Cuyayamahuit	1
Espada, 12	Siguigaimucita	1
Pedernales, 12	Noct?	1
Total 1784		

COMMENTARY. Goycoechea expresses the opinion, based on what the Gentiles tell him, that the pagans do not get baptized because if they did, they would have to live in the mission and would not be able to continue their lifestyles of fishing and hunting.[74]

APRIL 15, 1796. Governor Borica writes to Goycoechea that he understands the hauling of wood for completion of the presidio chapel began on April 4.[75]

COMMENTARY. This apparently refers to the lengthening of the chapel from its original interior length of 54 feet to 99 feet.

JULY 27, 1796. Governor Borica writes to Goycoechea saying that he should have 10,000 bricks made for a pottery kiln, and that as soon as the potter in Monterey is finished with his

---
[74]State Papers, Missions, II, 229-33.
[75]Provincial Record, IV, 331.

work, he will be transferred to Santa Barbara.[76] Shortly thereafter, Goycoechea reports the kiln is under construction.

JANUARY 4, 1797. Governor Borica writes to Goycoechea that he is pleased that on the day of La Guadalupe [the feast day of Our Lady of Guadalupe is December 12th] the presidio chapel will be consecrated.[77]

APRIL 10, 1797. Goycoechea acknowledges receipt of a memo from Governor Borica warning that each presidio should put itself in a state of alert against invasion by the English. In compliance with this warning, Goycoechea has posted a sentry from dawn to dusk on a high ridge close to the beach near La Purísima Mission, and another at Ortega's ranch at Refugio Canyon, another at Mission San Buenaventura and one at the Domínguez Ranch near Los Angeles. The troops are given daily drill in the handling of arms. Goycoechea has decided against placing any battery of cannon on the beach at Santa Barbara because for the 6-caliber cannon, there are only 118 cartridges with the balls and there is no gunner and few troops to service it. Also, to train a cannon on the anchoring ground would be useless, since the English could land anywhere along the coast and attack the presidio from the landward side.[78]

COMMENTARY. France declared war against Britain, Holland and Spain early in 1793, and invaded Spain in 1794. In July 1795 Spain signed a peace treaty with France, and in August 1796, Spain allied itself with France against Britain. Spain's colonies were aware of the possibility of invasion by the English all during these years.

JUNE 19, 1797. Goycoechea reports to Governor Borica the arrival of a master blacksmith who is to repair the armaments and perform similar work.[79]

SEPTEMBER 8, 1797. Mission San Fernando Rey was

[76]Provincial Record, IV, 348-49.   [77]Provincial Record, IV, 363.
[78]Provincial State Papers, XV, 240-42.   [79]Provincial State Papers, XV, 266.

founded by Fr. Fermín Francisco de Lasuén on the Reyes Rancho in San Fernando Valley. He was accompanied by Sergeant Ignacio Olivera and five soldiers from the Santa Barbara Presidio.[80] By October 4th, the guardhouse and storehouse had been completed and construction of two houses had begun.

DECEMBER 14, 1798. Goycoechea wrote to Governor Borica responding to fifteen questions posed by the Viceroy. These responses tell us much about the daily life at the presidio, a subject for future research.[81]

DECEMBER 31, 1798. Goycoechea sends to Governor Borica a listing of all the members of the Santa Barbara Presidio Company, a total of sixty-two soldiers, plus the names of seven *inválidos*, or retired soldiers, living in the area.[82]

COMMENTARY. Summarizing the data presented above, we find that construction of the buildings in the first (southeast) side of the quadrangle took from June 14, 1784, to sometime in July 1786, about two years. However, adobes for the second facade were being made during this period, and probably the foundations for the second side were being laid as early as February 1786.

By December 1786, the second side of the quadrangle had been completed and the families had moved into their homes. Six months later, in June 1787, the original fifty-four foot long chapel had been completed, and one year later, the fourth side had been erected, leaving only the exterior defense wall to be constructed.

Construction of the outer defense wall took almost three and a half years to complete. It was four feet thick and approximately nine feet high. We do not know if it was of solid adobe blocks or if only the outer faces were adobe and the interior was filled with mud or stone. As early as August 1793, it was recognized that the presidio chapel was too small for the population and needed lengthening. This was accomplished by the day of its dedication, December 12, 1797, and probably took about a year.

---

[80]Engelhardt, *Mission San Fernando Rey*, p. 10; Provincial State Papers, XVI, 247.
[81]Provincial State Papers, XVII, 71-80.
[82]Provincial State Papers, Benicia Military, XVII, 324-25.

Chapter Eight

Materials of Construction

As soon as man became nomadic and abandoned the comfort and safety of natural shelters such as caves, he had to learn how to build artificial habitations. The materials used to build these shelters varied throughout the world. In forested areas, he used wood and leaves, with vines holding parts together. As he became more civilized, he built with stone and other more stable materials. Where stone and wood were in short supply, shelters were built with earth and where grass grew thick, of sod. In freezing climates, blocks of snow were used.

The Chumash, the native Indians of the Santa Barbara area, built their hemispherical huts with poles stuck in the ground in a circle and bent over and joined at the top. The structure was then made relatively waterproof with grasses and leaves secured with reeds and vines. Some of these huts housed as many as fifty people. One advantage of this type of construction was that as soon as it became untenable because of age and vermin, it could be burned down and a new one built quickly elsewhere.

The earliest structures built by the Spanish in California were of "palisade" construction—posts set vertically in the ground, flat roofs covered with brush, leaves and dirt, and all surfaces plastered with mud to keep out the cold and weather. Such buildings provided temporary shelter and protection. As soon as possible, and after they were reasonably safe from attack, they commenced permanent structures using the materials and methods with which they were familiar in Mexico, Baja California and the Southwest.

Their materials were stone, adobe, mortar, fired brick and tile, wood beams and door and window frames, rawhide, a limited amount of metal, and later, glass.

STONE

Where stone was needed in the construction of the presidio, the builders had little variety near at hand. Sandstone was and is the only native stone readily available in quantity in the Santa Barbara area, and it appears in all sizes, from small boulders to rock ledges. None were available on the surface at the presidio, but they were easily hauled in from the foothills, from nearby creeks and from the seashore. Many of the stones and boulders uncovered in the foundations of the presidio buildings and walls were pitted with the holes of shellfish. Similar stones can be found along the beaches of Santa Barbara County.

As far as we know, stones were used only in the foundation trenches of the buildings and walls of the presidio, at least at first. An 1855 painting of the Presidio Chapel shows what could be a stone facade around the front door of the chapel, but it has been concluded it is of *ladrillos*, or baked floor tiles (see figure 7, page 137). Other than Private Rosalio, we have no record that any of the early soldiers were stonemasons, nor that a stonemason was brought to the presidio as an artisan.[1] Anyone familiar with the wizardry of the Italian stonemasons brought in at a later date, who were able to determine the grain of a boulder and split it with a chisel to obtain a flat facing, will realize that any appreciable quantity of stonework would have required a skilled stonemason.

---

[1] Since this was written, new information about skilled artisans and craftsmen working in Alta California has been discovered. *See* Mardith Schuetz Miller, *Building and Builders in Hispanic California 1769-1850*, (Tucson, 1995). Ed. note.

While the stones on the outside edges of the top section of the foundations have flat outside surfaces, they appear to be uncut. In all probability the workmen selected stones with one flat surface for the exposed portions of the foundations.

Santa Barbara now has a remarkable array of structures built of sandstone—houses, walls, curbstones, hitching posts, gate posts, fountains, etc., but these were mostly constructed in the latter half of the nineteenth century.

ADOBE

According to the *Encyclopaedia Britannica, adobe* is a Spanish word derived from the Arabic word *atob* meaning "sun-dried brick." In California it usually is associated with a dark, heavy, gummy soil which, as gardeners know, sticks like glue to a person's shoes in wet weather, but readily flakes off on a clean carpet when dry.

The best soil for making durable adobe bricks is a sandy loam.[2] A high percentage of sand causes crumbling of the bricks. Too much clay causes shrinking and cracking. The predominant soil of the Santa Barbara Presidio area is adobe. As the contractors who dig utility trenches and building foundations will testify, no native stones exist in the top six to eight feet in that area.

Structures made of adobe bricks had many advantages, among them being: availability of the material close to the building site, cheapness and simplicity of construction, rooms that are warm in winter and cool in summer, immunity to attack by rats or termites, natural fireproofing and sound proofing, and an attractive texture that can readily be painted. The primary disadvantages are susceptibility to damage by earthquake and the necessity of protecting exterior surfaces from erosion by storms, both by a moisture-proof roof and by plastering on the outside. Modern construction utilizes

---

[2] J. D. Long, *Adobe Construction*, pp. 24-27.

petroleum products or bitumals or cement as an admixture to prevent erosion, and concrete and reinforcing steel as insurance against damage from earthquakes. Absence of these materials in the mission period accounted for frequent structural failure.

Adobe bricks were made by the Indians for the Spanish in pits or troughs of appropriate size dug into the ground where the consistency of the soil was suitable.[3] Water was added to create a fairly stiff consistency. The requirement of water often dictated the location of the pit near a stream, lake, well or aqueduct.

After adding straw, grass, pine needles, manure, weeds, or similar binding materials, the Indians, stripped to a minimum of clothing, jumped into the pit and jogged the combination until it was thoroughly mixed. The mud was then scooped out into dampened wooden molds set out on a level piece of ground. The dimensions of the mold were usually convenient fractions of one *vara* (33 inches). Generally, the length of a brick in the Santa Barbara Presidio structures was ⅔ of a *vara* (22"), the width ⅓ of a *vara* (11"), and the thickness about ⅛ of a *vara* (4"). These were the approximate dimensions of bricks in the second defense wall of the Santa Barbara Presidio found in place under the building at 915 Santa Barbara Street. Such a brick, weighing 50 to 60 pounds, can be readily lifted and moved around. Other dimensions, such as ½ *vara* (16½") by ¼ *vara* (8 ¼") can be found in some old Santa Barbara adobe buildings.

The molds had neither top nor bottom, only the four sides. After the molds were filled, the mud was tamped, the top surface leveled smooth, and the mold lifted off. After drying in place for a day or two, the bricks were set on edge to dry more thoroughly on all sides. In a couple of weeks or more,

---

[3]Webb, *Indian Life at the Old Missions*, p. 105.

depending on the weather, the bricks were dry enough to stack in piles adjacent to where the walls were to be built.

According to J.N. Bowman, who has written on adobe construction,

> an Indian would often leave an impression of his hand or foot on the surface of a freshly packed brick, or a literate workman would print his name and the date on the surface. Sometimes a domestic or wild animal or bird would leave a footprint on the adobe before it dried.[4]

If the Indian children assigned to guard the adobes from wandering dogs and turkeys were alert, these autographs were missing. Even now Mexican floor tiles purchased for patios have the imprint of a hand or a chicken's claws, and these are prized products.

In 1799, Governor Borica instructed his four presidio commanders to obtain information on fifteen questions, one of which directly concerned construction. The reply by Commandant Goycoechea reflected adversely on the Franciscan Fathers, which in turn brought heated response.[5] Incensed, Fathers Estevan Tapis and Juan Cortés of Santa Barbara Mission refuted negative statements in a long *Respuesta*, or reply, so detailed that it has given us one of the best available descriptions of certain activities of that period. The key question (No. 9) which concerned construction was: How many hours are the Indians made to work? Are pregnant women and those nursing children, and the aged women and children, obliged to work?

Part of Tapis's reply tells us much about the making of adobes at the Presidio:

> Men make the adobes [at the Mission]. Nine men will make three hundred and sixty adobes a day, which is forty for each one. The soil

---

[4]Bowman, "Adobe Houses of the San Francisco Bay Region," pp. 57-64.
[5]Engelhardt, *Missions and Missionaries of California*, vol. II, pp. 566-600.

is soft and water is nearby. Those who work at this task never labor
after eleven o'clock in the morning, and never on Saturdays, nor
many times on Fridays, because during the first days of the week
they have accomplished the task for the last days, and are then
free...

Now let us compare the tasks of making adobes and tiles at the
mission with those at the presidio... With regard to the number of
adobes which should constitute an Indian's task for a day, Governor
Arrillaga in 1793 fixed the number at fifty. Last year, Sergeant José
M. Ortega asked for Indians from the missions to make adobes to
build his house outside the presidio. He was warned that the task
must not exceed fifty adobes for each Indian. He agreed to the condition, but he took it upon himself to enlarge the mould [sic] considerably. In addition, the water had to be drawn from a well more
than twelve yards deep.[6]

It has been estimated that the Goycoechea plan for the
Presidio required the manufacture of somewhere in the
neighborhood of 260,000 adobes. At fifty adobes per day per
Indian, that meant 5,200 man-days of work. Elsewhere it
was stated that the Indians worked from two hours after sun-
rise (say 8 A.M.) to 11:15, at which time they ate the noon
meal. In the afternoon they worked about an hour and a half.
If ten Indians were working at a time making adobes for a
project, and assuming, as is indicated by Father Tapis, that
they did not work on Saturdays and Sundays, it would take
the ten men 104 weeks or two years to make all the adobes for
the Presidio. Since as many as eight weeks in a year would be
so wet that adobe making would not be practicable, we can
assume that the manufacture of just the adobes for the Presidio probably took about two and a half to three years.

Mortar

The *Encyclopaedia Britannica* defines mortar as a mixture
of inert siliceous material (sand) with cement, which hardens

[6]Engelhardt, *Missions and Missionaries of California*, II, 576-77.

to a stonelike mass when mixed with water. The uses of mortar as an adhesive to bind stones to each other in building construction were known to the ancient Egyptians, Romans and Greeks. The cementing material used in the mortar of the presidio and mission structures to bind stones together was lime instead of cement, but adobe structures normally used adobe mud as the mortar between adobe bricks. Lime mortar does not bond well with adobe. The method by which lime plaster was made to stick to vertical wall surfaces will be explained further on.

When the underpinnings of the Bonilla House at 915 Santa Barbara Street were replaced and reconstructed in 1973, the stone foundations of the second defense wall of the presidio were uncovered. Several courses of the original adobe brick remained on top of the foundations. Although the wall was faced with a stucco of plaster, no lime plaster was observed in the joints between bricks. Adobe mud had been used as a mortar in the joints and the weight of the adobe wall had compressed the mud so that the horizontal joints were almost invisible. Vertical joints were about one to one and a half inches wide, and since no compression had occurred, the mortar could easily be scraped out. Where the construction required a bond that would uniformly distribute the weight of the structure over an uneven surface, such as stone, or provide a stronger adhesive joint between stones, lime mortar was used. Mortar also was used to plaster the outside of the building to eliminate erosion. Goycoechea's report accompanying his plan of 1788 states that "the front walls of the first front are standing; they are one and a half adobes [bricks] thick, mortared because of the poor quality of the soil for adobes."[7]

Limestone is predominantly calcium carbonate. It is found

---

[7]Provincial State Papers, XII, 61.

in small deposits in the Channel area and in large beds in the Santa Ynez Valley. Seashells such as were found along Santa Barbara beaches, and in large quantity in the shell mounds of the Indian villages, are also predominantly calcium carbonate. When either of these substances is heated (calcinated) to a high temperature, carbon dioxide is expelled and a dry, powdery substance called quicklime results. The limestone, lime shale or seashells are normally broken up into small pieces before heating. To make quicklime usable as a mortar, water is added (called slaking) to produce hydrated lime. The slaking process produces heat, and steam may escape when the process is rapid. Normally slaked lime is allowed to stand in putty-like form for a day or longer before using. Lime putty alone shrinks excessively when it sets or hardens. To prevent or reduce the cracking caused by shrinking, sand or clay is added. Beach sand can be used, but fresh water sand provides a stronger bond. According to Edith Webb, the lime plaster used to protect exterior walls was prepared by mixing three or four parts of lime to one of sand and water. She also described the use of the liquid from fleshy cactus pads as an adhesive and water repellent in the plaster and whitewash.[8]

The cactus used for this purpose was, according to Edward K. Balls, the tuna or prickly-pear (*Opuntia occidentalis*), an import into California from Mexico.[9] This use did not occur in the early period of the Presidio, but after the Mission was established the plant was used as a hedge surrounding corrals and other installations. It is found in great quantity at La Purísima Mission. To this day, sighting a patch of prickly pear in the general neighborhood of a mission indicates the possible remains of an outpost of mission activity.

Beach sand was used in the mortar of presidio structures. Father Tapis's *Respuesta* says that the Indians making adobes

---

[8]Webb, *Indian Life at the Old Missions*, p. 107-08.
[9]Balls, *Early Uses of California Plants*, pp. 35-36.

and tile at the Presidio "had to fetch the sand from the beach one-eighth of a league [1,700 feet] away."[10]

A visitor to the Presidio in 1827, A. Duhaut-Cilly, tells us where the lime was obtained for making mortar at the mission. In his account of the hardships of obtaining construction materials, he writes that the workmen had "to gather at great expense on the seashore, shells to make into lime."[11]

In the writings of another visitor in 1844, Eugene Duflot de Mofras, appears a general statement pertaining to construction materials at California missions:

> Lime was made either by burning limestone, which, although not of the best quality, was obtainable, or by burning sea-shells, of which there was a never-failing supply. Since all wall surfaces, inside and out, were kept whitewashed, lime was necessary at all times, and it is to be guessed that the burning of sea-shells, furnished the greater part of it.[12]

In specifically describing Mission Santa Barbara, he states that "in the mountains [there] are calcareous shell deposits which are used for building," as a source of lime.

John P. Harrington, the archaeologist who excavated the Indian village of Yananolit *(Shuktu)* at Burton Mound, is quoted by Browne as follows:

> The cement that the Spaniards and *padres* used to make was very hard. It is still to be seen at the Missions. You can hardly break it with a pick or crowbar. They got the rock for making the cement here in the Lulapin country. They prepared it a year before they wanted to use it. It had to lie as long as that in order to have the proper qualities. The cement was made of *arena* (sand) and *cal crudo* (raw lime). The lime was burned in kilns in the Lulapin country. The kilns were round like a tall furnace. There was one kiln where the Jennings place is in Ventura river canyon. A kiln above Santa Inez was used only for making tile and brick. At Santa Barbara

---

[10]Engelhardt, *Missions and Missionaries of California*, II, 578.
[11]Carter (trans.), "Duhaut-Cilly's Account of California," p. 160.
[12]Wilbur (trans. & ed.), *Duflot de Mofras' Travels*, vol. I, p. 195.

there was a kiln down toward the Potter hotel at the place owned by the old man Cavalleria. This was for *cal*. This lime was used quick. They calculated how much was wanted for a structure and mixed it with sand and added no water. They allowed it to lie dry, first covering it with a coat of dry sand. They let it lie thus so that the lime would cure the sand. Later they would uncover a part of it and try it, and put water on, and try it. A man once offered to pay Fernando much money for the secret of making this cement which he is telling us now. To test the cement, they half-baked a big leaf of cactus, and mashed it (the leaf) and put it in a vessel, and put water on it and let it stand for five days. That makes the gummy part mix with the water and it becomes hard. After a little cement is mixed with the water in order to try it, they would take a brick or adobe and cement it to another one and let it dry. If the cement does not crack it is O.K. If it cracks more sand must be added. If O.K., they brush over the face of the cement with some tuna water and the job was fine. The kind of tuna (cactus) used in connection with the cement was called *V. siepo*.[13]

Webb describes the construction and operation of lime kilns as follows:

Lime kilns were constructed of adobe bricks and, wherever possible, were built against a hillside to permit of easy dumping of limestone, raw lime, or sea-shells into the kiln from above. Mr. F. E. Green says: "In size and shape these kilns at San Diego Mission are all quite similar, and like the early kilns at other places up and down the coast. A bottle shaped opening was dug in the hillside from seven to fifteen feet in depth and five to eight feet in diameter, with the top and bottom slightly contracted, and sometimes curbed with brick or stones around the top, and rarely all the way to the bottom... The preparation of the kiln for a run required that a full supply of the necessary fuel should be gathered, and also the necessary amount of raw lime material be brought to the top of the kiln. Then the kiln was filled with alternate layers of fuel and lime-rock and fired, adding more fuel if necessary to obtain the desired temperature. From two to five days would be required in the burning and cooling process."[14]

---

[13]Robert O. Browne, "San Buenaventura Water System," MS, 1974, report, pp. 63-64.
[14]Webb, *Indian Life at the Old Missions*, p. 106.

A lime kiln was constructed at an early date on the bank of the creek that flows through Hope Ranch. High above the opposite bank is a quarry from which limestone was excavated for the kiln. The adjacent road is called La Cantera (stone quarry). A large chunk of calcite was found there on a recent visit, but informed sources say the main purpose of the quarry, at least during this century, was to provide material for road fills in the neighborhood.

A newspaper article dated June 26, 1975, reports the finding of a lime kiln in the Chatsworth Reservoir area about ten miles from San Fernando Mission. The structure, composed of a circular, rock-lined pit at the edge of a low cliff, is fifteen feet deep and has a diameter of seven feet. According to anthropologists, workers cut the branches from the tops of oak trees. These were dumped into the kiln along with lime and burned with extreme temperatures to produce a lime ash. Many of the rocks lining the kiln have become vitrified —glassy smooth as a result of melting from the heat.[15]

WHITEWASH

Again drawing upon the often utilized *Encyclopaedia Britannica* for definition and enlightenment, we find that whitewash is a water paint used mainly for decorative purposes. Richard Henry Dana, in 1835, notes that the Mexican flag was flying from the little square whitewashed Presidio.[16] Earlier visitor British Captain George Vancouver described the Santa Barbara settlement buildings as being "regular and well constructed, the walls clean and white, and the roofs of the houses were covered with bright red tile."[17]

If an adobe building was properly constructed, it had a plastered exterior of lime mortar as a means of preventing

---

[15]*Los Angeles Times*, Thursday June 26, 1975, Part VII.
[16]Dana, *Two Years Before the Mast*, vol. I, p. 97.
[17]Wilbur (ed.), *Vancouver in California*, vol. II, p. 150.

erosion of the adobe blocks in wet weather. Such a coating provided a smooth surface ideal for whitewashing as a beautification project. But the whitewash itself, if prepared with cactus juice as previously described, had some value in repelling water.

If a thick paste or jelly is made by mixing lime with water and a glue or size, the resulting liquid is variously known as whitewash, distemper, or, in a dry state, calcimine. The glue or sizing was furnished by the cactus juice. The end result was a paint which would wash off or flake off, hence the walls required continuous maintenance. The addition of oil or varnish improved durability.

Edith Webb cites a Mexican worker who made his whitewash by mixing lime with goats' milk and a little salt. With characteristic thoroughness, she experimented with these ingredients and produced a soft, smooth whitewash that was relatively durable. It also, she reports, provided an excellent surface for mural decoration such as probably existed in the interior of the Presidio chapel.[18]

WOOD

In his description of the Santa Barbara area in August 1769, Father Juan Crespí, diarist of the Portolá expedition, mentioned the prevalence of live oaks, alders and willows, and said that "on the summits [of the Santa Ynez range] there are some pines."[19]

Archibald Menzies, the botanist who accompanied Vancouver on his visit to Santa Barbara in November 1793, stated:

In the woody clumps to the Westward of the Presidio there are some Poplar [*Populus trichocpa* or Black Cottonwood] and American Plane Trees [*Platanus racemosa* or Western Sycamore] but they

---

[18]Webb, Indian *Life at the Old Missions*, p. 108.
[19]Bolton, *Crespí*, p. 166.

are mostly composed of the evergreen oak already mentioned which grow to pretty large trees, though not handsome in appearance, they might however answer for Timber in building small vessels as the wood of this Oak was found on trial pretty good, our Carpenters having worked up some of it for the ship's use.[20]

Richard Henry Dana states that the low plain of Santa Barbara was covered with grass but entirely without trees. He undoubtedly overlooked those in arroyos and was comparing Santa Barbara's native vegetation with that of more northern, forested regions.[21]

Oaks of the type found in the Santa Barbara area, primarily the California Live Oak (*Quercus agrifolia*) at lower levels and the Canyon Live Oak (*Quercus chrysolepis*) at higher levels, made poor construction lumber because of their short trunks and branching habits, but they made good firewood for the early explorers and, of course, the acorns were a dietary staple for the Indians. The California Live Oak was called "the holly-leaf oak" by early explorers. The Spanish called these evergreen oaks *los encinos*. The deciduous oaks found in the Santa Ynez River valley were called *los robles*.

The Western or California sycamore (*Platanus racemosa*), also called cottonwood, found generally along creeks, grows to a height of up to ninety feet and three to six feet in diameter. It produced some long timbers but branches are generally twisted and bent. Slices through the trunks are said to have been used for the wheels of *carretas*, the ox-drawn, noise-polluting (unless axles were greased every few minutes) carts which were the only practical means of transporting heavy loads.[22] The Sailors' Sycamore, which stood until recently at Quinientos and Milpas streets in Santa Barbara, was said to be more than 200 years old;[23] but the life of untreated

---

[20]Wilbur (ed.), "Menzies' California Journal," p. 320.

[21]Dana, *Two Years Before the Mast*, I, 61.

[22]Phillips, *History of Santa Barbara County*, p. 65.

[23]Muller, Broder & Beittel, *Trees of Santa Barbara*, p. 163.

sycamore lumber under exposed conditions is perhaps as short as five years. Hence when used at the Presidio or Mission, it had to be replaced frequently. It is described as moderately hard, moderately heavy, moderately strong and difficult to split. It shrinks moderately and is inclined to warp in seasoning. The Spanish word for this wood is *sicomoro*.

Another source of structural lumber was the white alder *(Alnus rhombifolia)* found along Santa Barbara streams in Mission, Rattlesnake and Sycamore canyons, and called in Spanish *aliso*.[24] These trees grow to a height of up to 75 feet with a diameter of 18 to 24 inches. Because the trunks are clear of branches for one-half to two-thirds of their length, they produce structural timber. Like the sycamore, the wood is not durable.

One more native tree possibly used for structural purposes was the Black Cottonwood (*Populus trichocarpa*), which has been known to reach a height of 125 feet and three to four feet in diameter. The wood is soft, straight-grained and fine-grained, although classified as a hardwood.

Most of the churches and chapels built during the later 1700s and early 1800s are long and narrow simply because tall timber for long beams to span wide churches was not available near the buildings. The interior width of the Presidio chapel dedicated in 1797 was 22 feet. The width of the third Santa Barbara Mission church was 26 feet. Kurt Baer states:

> Wood was used as a construction material in some places more than others. Pine was the most common wood, it was preferred because of its usually straight grain, the ease with which it could be cut, and its apparent greater durability. In several missions, roof beams and other supports originally made from poplar and alder, which grew profusely in the canyon areas, were replaced with pine. "Because they were decayed and therefore dangerous...all the buildings of

---

[24]Sudworth, *Forest Trees of the Pacific Slope*, pp. 263-66.

the mission [Santa Barbara] have pine wood throughout," states
the annual report of December, 1796. The rafters and many beams
were originally of sycamore and cottonwood.[25]

Pine trees were not native to the Santa Barbara plain. One
can still see the pines in the vicinity of La Cumbre Summit
that were noted by Father Crespí in 1769, but it is unlikely
that they were used at the Presidio or at the Mission because
of the roughness of intervening terrain. Yet Duhaut-Cilly
commented concerning his visit to the Santa Barbara Mission in March 1827 that:

> the construction of this edifice would have been nothing to excite
> surprise, had it been built by Europeans... Here, on the contrary,
> everything is in the rough, even the men... The first care of the
> builder has been to form his workmen. Out of the mere earth he
> has had to make bricks and tiles; to cut immense trees far away, and
> to bring them, by physical strength, over roads marked out
> expressly across ravines and precipices...[26]

The location of the stands of pine used in Mission Santa
Barbara and possibly in the Presidio is unknown, but it could
have been the San Rafael range north of the Santa Ynez
River, where the Coulter Pine (*Pinus coulteri*), the Digger
Pine (*Pinus sabiniana*) the Jeffrey Pine (*Pinus jeffreyi*), the
Western Yellow Pine (*Pinus ponderosa*), the Single-leaf Pine
(*Pinus monophylea*) and the Sugar Pine (*Pinus lambertiana*)
are native. If pines were obtained from that great a distance,
one must admire the fortitude of the Indians who performed
this feat, probably on their shoulders. Undoubtedly the trees
were felled and the timbers adzed to reduce their weight
before hauling or carrying them to Santa Barbara. Father
Geiger says merely that:

> in 1796 the Fathers discovered that throughout the buildings all
> the beams of sycamore and poplar had become rotted. These had to

[25]Baer, *Architecture of the California Missions*, p. 21.
[26]Carter (trans.), "Duhaut-Cilly's Account of California," p. 157.

be replaced with pine timber which had to be hauled from a distant mountain range.[27]

This was only two years after this particular church, the third since 1786, had been dedicated.

In March 1786, *Comandante* Goycoechea informed Governor Fages that "this same weak wood will be cut for the roofs."[28] It seems likely, therefore, that wood for the Presidio buildings, probably pine, was shipped down from Monterey on orders of the governor. The missions apparently did not have this cooperation from the governor. Also at variance with the assumption that lumber for the Presidio came from local sources are documentary statements. Under date of July 7, 1785, *Comandante* Goycoechea reports that Private Francisco Ruiz is in Monterey cutting wood.[29] On August 1, 1785, the Governor, in answer to a request from Goycoechea for wood, said he will send what he can, but that Goycoechea should send two or three woodcutters every two months to cut it.[30] In June 1786 Goycoechea informed the Governor that Captain Martínez of the frigate *Princesa* delivered 58 beams and 12 girders, presumably shipped in from Monterey.[31]

Monterey was a convenient source of pine because groves grew, and still grow, so close to the port. Captain Alejandro Malaspina, whose scientific expedition visited Monterey in September 1791, had with him trained personnel who reported on the availability, qualities, and uses of the timber in the Monterey area, including fifteen different varieties.[32] From these descriptions it appears that the major portion of

[27]Geiger, *Mission Santa Barbara, 1782-1965*, p. 42.

[28]Provincial State Papers, VI, 319.

[29]*Archivo General de la Nación, Obras Públicas, tomo* 15, 1784-1803.

[30]Provincial State Papers, V, p. 223.

[31]Provincial State Papers, VI, 307-08.

[32]Cutter, *Malaspina in California*, pp. 78-80.

the wood used for structural purposes in the Presidio was Monterey Pine.

WATTLES

The description of the Santa Barbara Presidio written by Goycoechea in 1788 indicates that certain buildings had roofs of beams, *estivas*, and roof tiles. The word *estiva* has been translated as "wattles" which, in turn, has been defined by *Webster's* as "rods laid on a roof to support the thatch" and "material consisting of wattled (twisted or interwoven) twigs, withes, etc. used for walls, fences, etc."

From photographs of old adobes, we know that pitched roofs were formed on roof rafters spaced two to four feet apart, on top of which were placed reeds or withes to span the distance between rafters and to support the roof tile. These reeds or withes would have had to be fairly thick and long to span several rafters and to support the heavy roof tile. In reconstructing the buildings at La Purísima Mission, the bamboo-like Giant Reed (*Arundo donax*) was used.[33] Probably by the time La Purísima Mission was rebuilt at the present site in 1813, this reed, which grows to a height of 18 to 20 feet, was available in quantity. It is unlikely, however, that it was available in the 1780s in sufficient quantity to have been used in the first tile roofs of the Santa Barbara Presidio. It seems more likely that the long slender branches of the native willow would have been used.

Webb notes that at San Juan Capistrano and San Luis Obispo Missions ceilings of carrizo, tule, saplings of what might be the elderberry bush, and willows were found.[34] Newcomb says that tule (*Scippus lacustris*) and cattail (*Typha latifolia*) had been in common use by the Indians and were

---

[33]Hageman and Ewing, *Mission La Purísima Concepción*, p. 90.
[34]Webb, *Indian Life at the Old Missions*, pp. 125-26.

therefore used in the *jacal* or Indian hut type of construction that was incorporated as part of the temporary "palisade" buildings.[35] The first buildings erected by Ortega at Santa Barbara were of this type of construction. Mud was used on the walls to seal cracks between reeds, and it is reported that *brea*, or asphalt, was used to seal the flat roofs. One of the inconveniences of this type of roof was the drip of melted tar on one's neck or head in the summer, the globs on the floor, and as a result, the leaking roof in the winter.

RAWHIDE

Ordinarily one would not consider the untanned hide of cattle or other animals as a building material. But just as baling wire was essential to maintenance of Model T's and farm machinery in the 1920s, so strips of rawhide found daily use as a one-piece repair kit during the Presidio period and later.

In 1861 William H. Brewer took a trip from Los Angeles to San Francisco. Just before reaching Carpinteria in March of that year, his party camped in Ventura County. His diary describes repairing the weak wagon wheel with that "universal plaster" for ailing implements, rawhide. He expressed surprise at the many uses to which rawhides could be put. In a house on a ranch, rawhide was spread before the beds as a carpet or mat. Bridle reins and ropes or lassos (*reatas*) were made of and fences were tied with it. Rawhide was the substitute for nails which, in the early days, were in extremely short supply.[36]

Robert G. Cleland quotes a traveler in Texas as writing:

> Rawhide slits the latch string, and the hinges, laces the shoes, lets the bucket down the well, weaves the chair, darkens one pane, twists the lariats, stretches the bedstead, is glue, nails, pegs and mortises. Rawhide is pegged to the ground to dry, rawhide is

---

[35]Newcomb, *The Old Mission Churches and Historic Houses of California*, p. 79.
[36]Brewer, *Up and Down California*, p. 48.

stretched across the yard to be oiled, rawhide is nailed across the house to grow pliable.[37]

Baer says:

> In all early descriptions of church construction one remarkable substitution is mentioned: rawhide thongs were used in place of nails and spikes to fasten together the *vigas* and other beams, especially in the roofing of churches. The rawhide, tightly wound and tied, shrank on drying and made a rigid joint. Remarkably unaffected by weather, many of the thongs lasted for a very long time...
>
> Rawhide also served as a substitute for glass for windowpanes. The skin was scraped very thin and was made translucent by numerous applications of oil. There is one such rawhide "window" at Mission San Miguel.[38]

The preparation and sale of hides and tallow later became a major industry in Alta California because of the huge herds of cattle. Tanning of hides was a three- to six-month process of soaking in a solution containing oak bark, the tannic acid of which changed the character of the hide to leather, which was then rubbed with oil, grease or tallow. Leather was used in making shoes, shields, the soldiers' leather jackets, sacks, buckets, saddles, bridle reins, and even doors, hinges and bell hangings.

Roof Tiles (*Tejas*) and Floor Tiles (*Ladrillos*)

The Spanish settlers in California learned at an early date that an adobe structure required a nonabsorbent roof that would rapidly shed water, otherwise rains melted the adobe walls and the structure failed. San Luis Obispo is generally credited with being the first California mission to be roofed with tile, but Mrs. Webb, who spent thirty years researching mission structures and writing one of the best reference books on the subject, refers to a statement in Fr. Junípero

---

[37]Cleland, *Cattle on a Thousand Hills*, p. 52.
[38]Baer, *Architecture of the California Missions*, pp. 25-26.

Serra's letter of December 8, 1781, to Father Lasuén regarding new missions.[39] After mentioning dedicatory services at San Carlos Mission, he wrote:

> I hope that before long it will rise up a fine building. Our church here [at Carmel] is to be slightly bigger—certainly no smaller. Until now, the Church of San Antonio [Mission] was ahead, especially for its tile roof.[40]

Mrs. Webb stated that the San Antonio roof of tile was constructed in 1780, two years before San Luis Obispo was roofed with tile. Prior thereto, all church roofs were of thatch, reeds and mud, and many roof fires occurred. At any rate, tile roofs were utilized prior to the founding of the Santa Barbara Presidio. Webb further wrote:

> In the making of tiles, as in the making of adobes, wooden molds were used. There is absolutely no truth in the story, often told and written, of the mission tiles having been molded on the Indians' thighs. There were two molds for the tiles, one being a shallow frame without top or bottom and wider at one end than at the other. The other was a rounded mold like a half-piece of log, or tree trunk, giving the tile the desired curve. One end of the mold was shaped smaller than the other, because, when laid on the roof, the larger end of the one tile fitted over the smaller end of the other previously laid. In an undated inventory taken at Mission San Francisco Solano, there are listed two wood *ladrillo* molds (2 *ladrilleras de madera*) and eight tile molds (8 *moldes de teja*).
>
> The writer witnessed the entire process of tile making, except the firing, at La Purísima, in 1937, when tiles were being made for the restored buildings. Mission-day methods were employed throughout the entire process, except with the mixing of the clay and other ingredients. For that operation, "Yankee ingenuity," it would have been called in bygone days, devised a more speedy and less strenuous method *a la máquina*.
>
> Preparatory to the molding of the tiles, a long bench, or table, had been arranged; the molds, or forms, were set and a bucket of

[39]Webb, *Indian Life at the Old Missions*, p. 108.
[40]Tibesar, *Writings of Serra*, IV, 99.

water set close by for use of the worker, who repeatedly dipped his hands into the water to keep them sufficiently wet for the proper handling and smoothing of the clay. When the clay was of the desired consistency, portions of it were thrown into the flat mold, firmly pressed down and into the corners by hand until the mold was completely filled. Any excess material was scraped off with a piece of board. The mold was then pulled to one end of the table, the form lifted by means of cleats nailed to the end pieces and the unfinished tile urged over the edge of the table onto the semi-cylindrical mold. This was a critical moment for it took some considerable skill to get the clay from the table to the mold without mishap. This feat was accomplished by holding the curved mold just below the edge of the table and turning it slowly as the clay was pushed over and onto it from above. The performance was perfect and the eyes of the youthful worker gleamed with satisfaction.

The mold with the clay on it was next placed back on the table and the tile maker, after once more wetting his hands, pressed the clay upon the mold, smoothed it, and then carefully trimmed its edges. It was now ready for the drying rack. There mold and clay were set—small end first—on a shelf of slats and the wooden form quickly jerked out by means of the handle attached to its larger end. If the clay mixture is of the proper consistency it will retain its curved shape without the form under it. It took many days for these tiles to dry, sometimes as long as a month, depending on the weather, of course. When thoroughly dry, they were fired, or burned, in the tile kiln and were then ready for use. None of the mission tile or lime kilns survive intact today, though the ruins of an almost complete one have recently been excavated at Mission San Luis Rey.

Ladrillos are made with a little stiffer, or heavier, mixture of clay than that required for roof tiles. The mixture for the latter must be pliable for molding over the curved form, but that for the *ladrillos* is thrown into a flat mold, tamped in, the frame lifted and the molded clay left to set before it is taken into the drying shed. Most clays need an admixture of sand to prevent cracking or excessive shrinking. Both roof and floor tiles shrink slightly in drying and firing...

Being handmade and imperfectly burned, the old tiles were more or less porous and in time lichens found lodging in their surfaces, giving to the roofs an even greater variation of color. Also, not being machine made, they varied in size and shape, a circumstance that gave to the roofs that uneven look that so delightfully suits the thick adobe walls beneath them.[41]

Ladrillos found at La Purísima Mission measured 10½" x 10½" x 2" and had the typical black core, indicating inadequate firing, found in *ladrillo* fragments at the site of the Santa Barbara Presidio chapel.

Father Tapis tells us how long it took to make tile. He wrote:

> Those who make tiles also have a certain number to make. Sixteen young men, and at times as many more middle-aged men, with two women who bring sand and straw, make 500 tiles a day. The troughs with the clay are close by and always filled. These neophytes accomplish their task before eleven o'clock in the morning, and always include the task for Saturdays likewise, on which they are then free to make excursions or to rest.[42]

As to the same kind of work at the Presidio, Engelhardt wrote:

> In 1795 *Comandante* Felipe de Goycoechea asked for ten Indians to make tiles. The most skillful and trustworthy were assigned for the task. Nearly all are still living. On the fourth day of work at the presidio, which was Thursday, they complained that they could not accomplish the work, and that their hands and arms ached them very much. They were asked what task they had performed that day. They replied they had made 500 tiles, but had to dig out the clay, throw it into the troughs, and draw water from a well fifteen yards deep or from a laguna some distance away. Moreover, they had to fetch the sand from the beach one eighth of a league away, procure the straw, knead the clay and from morning till night they had to work, because a soldier stood by who saw that the 500 tiles were made. This seemed almost incredible, and we feared that the Indians were lying. Nevertheless, they were consoled and encouraged to continue the work. On Friday night they repeated their complaint with more vehemence, and declared they had on that

---

[41]Webb, *Indian Life at the Old Missions*, pp. 108-10.

[42]Engelhardt, *Missions and Missionaries of California*, II, 577.

day made 525 tiles. They were told to be patient, to try once more, and steps would be taken to relieve them of such hardship. On Saturday *Comandante* Goycoechea came to the mission and was told of the complaints of the Indians. He replied that such was the task which the soldiers had formerly accomplished. It was then proposed to him to put the ten best soldiers to work with ten Indians in order to see which party laboring from morning till night made the most tiles. To this he would not agree. However, he said he had enough tiles now, and needed the Indians no longer.[43]

PIGMENTS AND PAINTS

This is a subject which could fill a book in itself. The Indians loved color and, in time, became reasonably proficient in its use in decorating mission structures. Some of the missions still retain the original Indian-executed paintings and mural designs but many were obliterated by well-intentioned restorers who failed to appreciate "primitives."

While there probably was little decoration in the Santa Barbara Presidio, Goycoechea's report dated September 16, 1788, describes the chapel as "lined with mortar and whitewashed... and adorned with painting."[44]

The Indians were users of pigments to paint their bodies, utensils, and other belongings long before the Spaniards arrived, and much has been written about the rock paintings of the Indians. Campbell Grant has written a section on pigments, techniques and styles in which he cites iron oxides, cinnabar from which quicksilver is derived, manganese, charcoal, and diatomaceous earth from Lompoc as origins for the pigments, while juices of plants and seeds, animal oils and whites of eggs, together with water, provided the binder.[45]

In an article on pigments used by the Mission Indians, Webb wrote at length on the subject. She points out that

---

[43]Engelhardt, *Missions and Missionaries of California*, II, 578-79.

[44]Provincial State Papers, XII, p. 60.

[45]Grant, *The Rock Painting of the Chumash*, pp.84-87.

memorias, or requisitions for supplies, from Mission Santa Barbara between 1797 and 1809 include several pigments and linseed oil, the latter being the binder.[46] Pigments used to decorate the walls of missions are also described in her book.[47]

METALS

Metals were valuable and rare materials during mission and presidio days. Since none were manufactured in California, all raw materials and fabricated items such as tools had to be shipped in from Mexico. The *Encyclopaedia Britannica* tells us that by the eighteenth century steel was in use and was manufactured by heating wrought iron with charcoal in a furnace, then bending, rolling and heating it. Its use, however, was pretty much limited to knives, weapons and tools.

In the annual report for San Diego Mission for 1777, it is stated that:

> San Diego Mission has furnished San Gabriel 41 pounds of iron and 23 ounces of steel, with the necessary charcoal, and a *peon* to fashion it for the various uses for which it has been offered. To San Juan Capistrano it...has supplied 20 pounds of iron and 16 ounces of steel, with adequate charcoal, and a *peon* for the work undertaken.[48]

The quantities involved vouch for the scarcity of these materials.

In a memorandum dated June 20, 1771, Father Junípero Serra noted that he had furnished two sheets of iron for the Monterey mission.[49] In March 1773, he complained to the Viceroy that only recently had San Diego Mission received a forge, that it had no blacksmith, and that only the Monterey

[46]Webb, "Pigments Used by the Mission Indians of California," p. 143.
[47]Webb, *Indian Life at the Old Missions*, pp. 231-44.
[48]Kenneally, *Writings of Lasuén*, II, 336.
[49]Tibesar, *Writings of Serra*, I, 229.

Presidio had a forge and a blacksmith.[50] Broken tools had to be sent to Monterey for repairs, sometimes taking a year. In 1774, Mission San Luis Obispo received four *arrobas* (about 100 pounds) of iron in bars. Slabs of lead also were shipped in. Most of these metals were used for tools and equipment such as plow points. The only use of metal as a construction material was the iron used for locks, keys, hinges, nails, hasps, hooks and similar small parts. Where possible, such as the grilles for windows, wood was substituted for metal.

Glass

Although glass was available in Mexico during the early days of the Presidio, it was too much of a luxury to ship to California due to its fragility. As previously mentioned, a substitute for window panes was found in thin and well-oiled rawhide. Windows were barred by wooden grilles, and wooden shutters hinged so that they swung inward from the frame to the splayed window opening.[51] Fragments of window glass were found in the ruins of the chapel of La Purísima Mission, built after the 1812 earthquake. Window glass must have been available to a limited extent by then.[52]

Reference to the use of glass is contained in a letter to Presidio *Comandante* José de la Guerra y Noriega dated September 27, 1821. In it Fr. José Señán, missionary at San Buenaventura and at that time President of the California missions, wrote:

> Enclosed are the measurements of the size of the broken windows of the Church and Sacristy and God willing Your Grace has some of them. Five of the large ones are missing and sixteen of the small ones. A leather sack is going along in case you can favor us with three or four of each kind of glass inside of it.[53]

---

[50]Tibesar, *Writings of Serra*, I, 315.

[51]Hageman and Ewing, *Mission La Purísima Concepción*, pp. 90-91.

[52]Hageman and Ewing, *Mission La Purísima Concepción*, pp. 92-93.

[53]De la Guerra Papers, folder 904, in Santa Barbara Mission Archive-Library.

In a letter to De la Guerra dated November 28, 1821, Father Antonio Peyri of San Luis Rey Mission expressed thanks for the information that Fr. Antonio Ripoll, missionary of the Santa Barbara Mission, will send him 50 panes.[54] As late as 1841 a visitor to Santa Barbara wrote: "Very few of the houses have glass windows. Open spaces in the walls, protected with bars of wood and plank shutters, serve instead."[55] Thus we know that window glass was available, though a prized commodity, but not whether it was used in Presidio windows.

---

[54]De la Guerra Papers, folder 777, in Santa Barbara Mission Archive-Library.
[55]Egenhoff, *Fabricas*, p. 61.

Chapter Nine

Methods of Construction

It is difficult to visualize the problems faced by builders of presidios and missions of the Spanish Southwest in the late eighteenth and early nineteenth centuries. Apparently artisans such as carpenters, stonemasons, blacksmiths and others skilled in construction techniques were not available in Alta California until the Viceroy answered Governor Fages's plea of September 1790 for skilled craftsmen plus teachers, millers and a surveyor. About twenty were sent from Mexico in 1792 and 1795, although some were not skilled in building techniques, but were shoemakers, tailors, potters, etc., who would teach the Indians their trades.[1] At first, regardless of whether their work was on presidios or missions, artisans' salaries were paid out of the Royal Treasury, but after 1795, all work done on the missions was paid for from the Pious Fund, a fund made up of contributions for evangelizing the Indians of California.[2]

Until these skilled workers arrived, the success of a building project, its durability, safety and beauty of form, depended primarily on the ingenuity, imaginativeness, common sense and experience, if any, of the priest or soldier in charge. Undoubtedly a deliberate effort was made by the top brass to include persons with construction experience in the roster of soldiers assigned to found and build a particular establishment. Pick any group of ten men today, and the

---

[1]Bancroft, *California*, I, 615.

[2]Tibesar, *Writings of Serra*, II, 475, note 97.

chances are that several will have a knack for figuring out how to go about erecting a structure.

This hit-or-miss, casual approach to building would not be tolerated now with its potentially lethal effect on occupants from structural failure, earthquake and fire, but in those days the alternative was to sleep in tents and hold church services in the open or to go home. Besides, the odds on injury and death by disease, hostile Indians, accident and old age were far greater than the unlikely collapse of a building on top of them.

Lack of training in architecture, lack of construction experience, absence of artisans to supervise and work with wood, stone and metal, and the fact that Indian labor was unskilled all combined to force adoption of an architectural style which Kurt Baer appropriately calls California Franciscan,[3] as contrasted with other Spanish Colonial styles incorporating more complex features.

The style was extremely simple, and the buildings of the Santa Barbara Presidio were the embodiment of that simplicity: tile roofs with relatively low pitch and overhanging eaves, thick adobe walls, wood beams and trim, and little ornamentation except the whitewashed walls and some painting in the chapel. There is no record that any persons designated strictly as artisans worked on Presidio structures, nor did the design demand those skills.[4]

No step-by-step description of the construction of a presidio or mission, written simultaneously, has been found to date. Ample evidence exists, however, not only to tell the methods of construction, but also the layout and appearance of almost the entire Presidio of Santa Barbara. This evidence is found in the documents describing progress in construction, in the archaeological excavations conducted on this and

---

[3]Baer, *Architecture of California Missions*, p. 14.
[4]See footnote 1, page 152, *ed. note.*

other sites, in adobe buildings of the period which have survived, and in descriptions of how buildings are constructed in Mexico where many techniques have remained unchanged for centuries. Evidence specific to the Santa Barbara Presidio is also found in the 1788 Goycoechea plan of the Presidio (see figure 9, page 191) and in the 1855 James Alden watercolor of the Presidio chapel (figure 7, page 137).[5]

Tools and Hardware

A wide variety of tools was available for construction of the Presidio. Mission inventories from the late 18th century contain axes, adzes, augers, hoes, nails, tacks, carpenter's squares, turner's lathes, planes, jointers, and tool boxes. Also listed are machetes in sheaths, bucksaws, hammers, pincers, soldering irons and solder, compasses, crowbars, forges and hammers, jack planes, saws, plumb-bobs, ropes, scales, trowels, drills and chisels. Hardware such as locks, hinges and crossbars for doors and windows are also listed.[6] Examples of many of these tools and items of equipment may be seen at some of the missions and in museums. Sketches of some of them, and descriptions of their use, are found in a book sponsored by the American Museum of Natural History.[7] Some of these items were not available except at a considerable distance. For example, in 1773 California had only one forge (at the Monterey Presidio) and one blacksmith. This caused a long delay in having tools repaired.[8] The annual report for the year 1779 prepared by Father Lasuén for San Diego Mission states that they had placed in the carpenter shop a square and a spirit level that came from Mexico.[9] At Purísima Mission, excavations in the 1930s unearthed saws, axes, mattocks, garden

---

[5]See footnote 43, page 105.
[6]Tibesar, *Writings of Serra*, I, 227-36 and II, 225-47, 279-83.
[7]Sloane, *A Museum of Early American Tools*.
[8]Tibesar, *Writings of Serra*, I, 315, 317.
[9]Kenneally, *Writings of Lasuén*, II, 344.

den tools, wood augers, leather tools and an obsolete tool formerly used for boring holes in adobe.[10]

DIMENSIONS

The standard unit of linear measurement for building in Spanish colonial times was the *vara*, sometimes called the Spanish yard and now generally accepted as equivalent to 33 inches or 2.75 feet.[11] For describing distances traveled, the league was used, the league being 2.6 miles or 13,728 feet. For short measurements, there was the *pulgada*, or Spanish inch, actually 0.92 inches or seven-eights of an inch, since there were 36 *pulgadas* to one *vara*. Fractional parts of a *vara*—a quarter, third, half, two-thirds and three-quarters—were used in such cases as the dimensions of an adobe brick or the thickness of a wall.

By comparing with measurements on the ground in excavated areas, it has been determined that the dimensions of the plan of the Presidio prepared by Goycoechea in 1788 were inside dimensions, from the inside of one wall to the inside of the opposing wall, rather than center-of-wall to center-of-wall. Thus, to determine the length of a row of attached buildings, the thickness of partition and end walls must be added to the length of the rooms as given by Goycoechea. Inside dimensions of the Presidio Chapel were given in the inventory prepared in 1855 when the Chapel was abandoned as a parish church in favor of Our Lady of Sorrows parish church.[12] Where the Goycoechea plan gives the height of a building, it is referring to the height from the ground to the top of the wall under the eaves.

One important point must be emphasized. The Spaniards lost no sleep over inaccurate measurements. They had no

[10]Hageman and Ewing, *Mission La Purísima Concepción*, p. 5.

[11]Bowman, "Weights and Measures of Provincial California," p. 334.

[12]*Inventorio de la Iglesia Parroquial de Santa Barbara*, circa 1856, in Santa Barbara Mission Archive-Library.

trouble establishing a straight line, but they did not always build to that line. Perhaps it is not just a legend that their measuring tapes were rawhide strips that were shorter in the morning when soaked with dew than in the afternoon when they dried out. In any event, few of the measurements shown on the Goycoechea plan are exact. They are "*mas o menos*" (more or less), and if the walls were not exactly straight, "*no importa*"—who cares?

FOUNDATIONS

After marking the inside and outside corners of a building or structure, probably using a carpenter's square to obtain right-angled corners, a line of rawhide, string, or rope was stretched between points to outline the foundation. A trench varying from one to three feet deep was then dug between the lines. It is unlikely that ordinary shovels were available to dig the trench; metals were too scarce and this tool has not been noted in the inventories.[13] The soil might have been loosened with an iron-shod plow pulled by oxen, then scraped out with a hoe or mattock, or perhaps shovels were carved out of wood. Soil removed from the trench would have been piled on both sides of the foundation so that the portion of the foundation extending above natural ground level would be supported until any cementing mortar had set and the foundation stones were tied together with adobe.

Sandstone boulders up to two feet in diameter were then hauled to the site in the shrilly squeaking *carretas*, or carts, pulled by oxen or mules. Most of the boulders found in excavated foundations came from nearby watercourses or from surface scatterings of stone washed down from the mountain outcrops. In the foundations at two locations, however, boulders contained holes bored by a species of shellfish, indicat-

---

[13]Shovels do appear in *memorias* (requisitions) and *facturas* (invoices) of the Santa Barbara Presidio discovered subsequent to this writing. *Ed. note.*

ing they were transported from the beach at least one mile distant.

The boulders were placed in the trench in as compact a pattern as possible and some effort was made to align flat surfaces along the edge of the trench. The interstices were partially filled with smaller stones, then mud was poured into the remaining gaps. Below natural grade, therefore, and within the confinement of the walls of the trench, the foundations were relatively solid, permitting little movement of the stones. The foundations were laid to a height of ten to eighteen inches above natural grade. Stones on the inner and outer face above the grade were either dressed to a flat surface, or stones naturally flat on one side were chosen, so that both edges of the foundations formed a fairly neat, straight line. Small stones and pieces of broken roof tile, intermixed with mud, were used to level off the top of the foundation to provide a smooth base upon which to start laying the adobe wall.

The depth and width of the foundation depended on the height and purpose of the wall it supported. The defense walls of the Presidio, presumably designed to withstand gunfire, were supported on foundations averaging about 46 inches in width, probably intended to be a *vara* and a third (44 inches) plus an overage to allow for the thickness of the joints between adobe blocks. They were about one *vara* (33 inches) deep; but based on the finding that the outside face was plastered from the top of the foundation down for about nine inches, it can be concluded that the foundations extended above natural grade at least nine or ten inches.

Exterior foundations of the Presidio Chapel were approximately 36 inches wide, a *vara* (33 inches) plus an overage for the joints in the adobes, and about 36 inches deep. In the excellent and detailed description of the Monterey Presidio written by Governor Fages and translated by Father Maynard Geiger, details are given of the first adobe church at Monterey whose foundations are of stone set in mortar:

These foundations extend two quarters [of a *vara* = 16½ inches] above the surface and are a *vara* and a half [49 ½ inches] in width. Upon these foundations rise the [adobe] walls five-fourths [of a *vara* or 41 inches] in thickness. The church is fifteen *varas* long, seven *varas* wide and seven *varas* high. The roof was flat.[14]

(For comparison, the original Santa Barbara Presidio Chapel was 20 *varas* long, 8 *varas* wide and 7½ *varas* high).

Later in the Fages report there occurs a description of the bell tower to the right of the chapel and the statement that:

this tower has its foundation of stone mortared with lime and protrudes from the ground for three-fourths of a *vara* (25 inches). The church and tower are plastered with lime within and without.[15]

Archaeological excavations have not progressed to the point where the thickness and depth of foundations of the residential structures can categorically be stated. From the data obtained at two sites, the padre's quarters and a foundation at 820 Santa Barbara Street, it can be assumed that the thickness of one-story residence foundations was 22 to 26 inches, or approximately two-thirds of a *vara* (22 inches). Their depth has not been determined at an undisturbed location, but is probably about two feet.[16] However, in a letter dated June 26, 1789, Goycoechea informed Fages of "having finished two facades which have been erected with about a half a *vara* of stone," implying a foundation 17 inches deep.[17]

As a matter of interest, the foundations of the La Purísima Mission residence building varied from two feet to four feet three inches in width, and one supporting a two-story parti-

---

[14]Geiger (trans. and ed.), "A Description of California's Principal Presidio, Monterey, in 1773," p. 328.

[15]Ibid., p. 328

[16]Subsequent archaeological investigation of the northeast corner of the Santa Barbara Presidio provides evidence for a width of approximately ⅔ *vara* or 2 feet for one-story residence foundations and depths of 9-24 inches below grade. *Ed. note.*

[17]Provincial State Papers, IX, 110.

tion was over seven feet in depth. Hageman notes that the walls were the same width as the foundation.[18]

An accurate survey to determine the elevations at various points of the bottom of the foundations of the Presidio Chapel revealed that they followed the slope of the land. In other words, when the trench for the foundations was dug, it was dug a uniform depth from the natural surface. As nearly as can be determined from early street profiles obtained from the City Engineer's office, the natural ground gradient sloped two percent lengthwise of the building. Any step-ups in the foundations occurred at partition walls.

In describing the foundations at Purísima Mission, Hageman states:

> The top of the stone work was, in general, adjusted to approximately six inches above floor lines, and the top was found to slope... the top of the foundation wall of the colonnade at the southwest end is three feet and ten and one half inches lower than the corresponding northeast corner. Since the columns were found to be of uniform height, it follows that the entire building was built on a gradient of slightly more than one percent. This was not unusual in California mission structures.
>
> The slope of the Workshops and Quarters building, adjoining the Residence, was found to be five feet in a distance of three hundred and twenty-three feet, or about one and one-half percent. The Church was found to drop but nine inches in its length of one hundred and seventy-four feet, or forty-three hundredths of one percent. Thus it appears that the controlling factor was the natural gradient of the site.
>
> Floors were adjusted to meet the slope, either with a step between rooms, or at times with a slight ramp. The floors themselves were made level, except for exterior walks and those in the corridor.
>
> In order to form an even surface to receive the first course of adobe brick, chips of roof tile, about two inches in diameter, or chips of flat stone of larger size were grouted in with mud.
>
> Despite the large proportion of mud mortar and rough character

---

[18]Hageman and Ewing, *Mission La Purísima Concepción*, pp. 83-84.

of the work, these foundations proved remarkably strong, and have remained in an excellent state of preservation. The great thickness of the walls, compared with modern work, reduces the proportionate square foot loading to safe limits.[19]

The foregoing descriptions apply to the second Purísima Mission, which was built after the earthquake of 1812, but there is no reason to assume that the construction techniques used then were any different from those used twenty-five years earlier during construction of the Santa Barbara Presidio. Based on the surveyed elevations of the foundations and the graves beneath the chapel floor, it appears that the original floor had a two percent slope. The extended Chapel nave had a length of 80 feet including the sanctuary or altar area. There is reason to believe the sanctuary was about 18 feet from front to back, leaving about 60 feet in the floor of the nave.

At the entrance to the Chapel, there were probably two or three steps up so that the nave floor was about one foot above the natural grade of the ground in order to provide proper drainage. The Chapel is the only long building parallel to the two percent slope. All other buildings probably also had at least one step at each door so that the floor was higher than the ground outside the building.

WALLS

The dimensions of adobe brick varied from place to place and even within one building. Webb states that the molds for making adobe averaged 11" x 23" x 4".[20] Hageman says a common size in early work was 10½" x 21" x 4", roughly ⅓ by ⅔ of a *vara*, but bricks 11" x 23" x 4" were used in the reconstructed La Purísima Mission.[21]

In the 1788 description of the Presidio prepared by

---

[19]Hageman and Ewing, *Mission La Purísima Concepción*, p. 84.
[20]Webb, *Indian Life at the Old Missions*, p. 105.
[21]Hageman and Ewing, *Mission La Purísima Concepción*, p. 85.

Comandante Goycoechea, he states that the thickness of the walls of the residences was three-fourths of a *vara*, plus the thickness of outside plaster, perhaps one inch each for the interior and exterior layers, for a total of 25 inches. As previously mentioned, however, measurements were not exact, and three-quarters of a *vara* was only an approximate dimension. Baer states that adobe bricks were generally 11" x 23" long and from 2" to 5" thick.[22] During the drying process, adobe bricks shrink, so that the end product may be somewhat smaller than the mold. It would seem logical that the builders would have used fractions of a *vara* in making their brick molds; thus a length of ⅔ *vara* (22 inches), a width of ⅓ *vara* (11 inches) and a thickness of ⅛ *vara* (4 ¼ inches).

The manner of laying up the adobe wall depended on the width of the wall, and the bricks were laid in patterns that would insure that no vertical joint continued from one course to the next. Possible patterns for different width walls are shown in figure 8.

Hageman notes:

> The practice of making the length of the brick slightly over twice the width is therefore a sensible one, since it works ideally for laying up the various thicknesses described with a maximum of bonding. Modern adobe bricks are generally made twelve by eighteen inches, which does not offer the same advantage.
>
> The mortar used was substantially the same soil as contained in the bricks except that it contained no straw. The average joint is about three-quarters of an inch—a course averaging throughout many measurements four and seven-tenths inches.[23]

When the underpinnings of the Bonilla House at 915 Santa Barbara Street were replaced, the foundations of the second defense wall were discovered, well protected by being under the house, and with several courses of adobe brick in

---

[22]Baer, *Architecture of the California Missions*, p. 18.
[23]Hageman and Ewing, *Mission La Purísima Concepción*, p. 85.

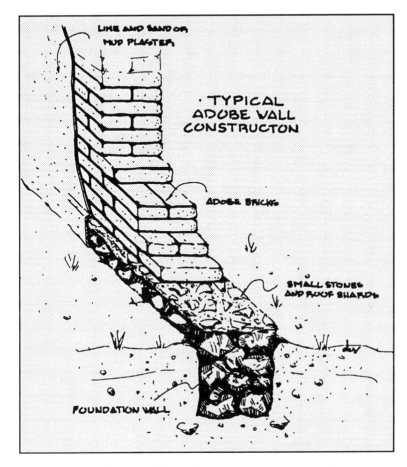

Figure 8: Typical adobe wall construction; reproduced from
Brian M. Fagan, *Archaeology of the Chapel Site*, Santa Barbara
Trust for Historic Preservation, 1976.

good condition on top of the foundation. The dimensions of
the bricks are approximately 11" x 22" x 4".

It was noted that the vertical joints were one to one and a
half inches wide, and that the mortar that filled the joint was

dried mud which could be scraped out with the finger. The horizontal joints, on the other hand, were virtually indistinguishable from the adobe bricks. Apparently the weight of the wall had so compressed the mortar that it blended in with the bricks. Only at the outer surface, where the corners of the brick were slightly rounded and the unsupported bonding mud had flaked off, was the pattern of horizontal joints apparent.

The southeast face of the outer defense wall was plastered with a lime-mortar layer about one inch thick to protect the wall from erosion in storms. At one point a layer of lime plaster six to eight inches in depth was found close to the wall, probably the remains of a mixing pit for the mortar.

The exact height of the walls of presidio structures is not known. Hawley gives the height of the defense wall as twelve feet, but he also gives the thickness of the wall as seven feet, a dimension disproved by archaeological excavations.[24]

A map of the entire Presidio in the files of the Santa Barbara Mission Archive-Library, drawn in pencil on heavy brown paper, also shows the outside wall (defense wall) as 12 feet high and 7 feet thick. A notation at the bottom of the map indicates the measurements are taken from Bancroft's *History of California*[25] and from measurements taken by Walter A. Hawley in 1895.[26] The probable explanation of the error in wall thickness is that Hawley measured the wall after the adobe had melted down and become a mound, rather than excavating down to the actual foundation stones. Hawley states in his preface that at the time of making the survey (in 1895) he consulted "a number of the oldest residents who are no longer living." Their memory may have been faulty. Unfortunately the whereabouts of the measurements taken by Haw-

[24]Hawley, *Early Days of Santa Barbara*, p. 35.
[25]Bancroft, *California*, I, 464-65.
[26]Hawley, *Early Days of Santa Barbara*, p. 35.

ley in 1895 are unknown. Possibly the map in the Mission Archives was made by Hawley, but this has not been proven.

A map of the Presidio from memory by Frank L. Birabent during his lifetime is now in the possession of his daughter, Mrs. Leontine Phelan of 820 Santa Barbara Street. This map shows the defense wall as eight feet high and three feet thick and capped with thatch.

De Mofras, speaking in general about the design of all presidios, says that "the rampart, or wall, constructed of adobes, was 4 or 5 meters high and a meter thick," which would make the defense walls 13 to 16 feet high and 39 inches thick.[27] It is very doubtful these proportions applied at Santa Barbara.

In August 1778, Governor Neve reported that he had reconstructed the Monterey Presidio with walls of stone four *varas* (11 feet) in height and one and one-third *varas* (3 feet 8 inches) thick.[28] In March 1792, Hermenegildo Sal, acting commander at San Francisco, reported that of the four defense walls, one was 4 *varas* high; one was 3 *varas* (eight feet) high; and two were 2½ *varas* (seven feet) high. He also reported many deficiencies which will be noted later. It would seem logical to assume that he intended all walls to be four *varas* high, and this seems a reasonable figure to use for the height of the Santa Barbara Presidio defense walls.[29]

In the letter to Governor Fages dated September 16, 1788, which contains the plans of the Santa Barbara Presidio, *Comandante* Goycoechea wrote that:

> of the thirteen houses shown on the fourth front of the quadrangle [the side in which El Cuartel is located] the walls are finished — three-quarters of a *vara* thick [25 inches] and three varas [8 feet, 3 inches] high without the ridge of the roofs, which are to be the same as the other houses for the soldiers...[30]

[27]Wilbur (trans. and ed.), *Duflot de Mofras' Travels*, I, 142.

[28]Provincial Records, I, 90.

[29]Provincial State Papers, XI, 236.

[30]Provincial State Papers, XII, 60.

At El Cuartel, the height from the floor to the top of the adobe wall is 8 feet, 7¼ inches; at the reconstructed Cañedo Adobe the wall height is 9 feet, 8⅜ inches.

The Goycoechea Plan of 1788 gives the height of the Chapel as 7½ *varas* or 20.6 feet. By relating the width of the front of the Chapel in the Alden painting of 1855 to the height of the eaves and roof ridge, it is obvious that the 20.6 feet is a measurement to the top of the wall under the eaves. Proportional to the width of the structure, the wall would be 19.1 feet high in the painting, a difference of 1.5 feet. The painting shows no steps at the entrance, but the calculations of the elevation of the Chapel floor assume that steps existed. By 1855 the level of the ground could have risen enough so that the steps were not in evidence. The difference of 1.5 feet might account for three steps up from natural ground level to the floor of the nave, but measurements taken from an early painting are not to be trusted.

Wall Openings

The Goycoechea Plan shows the number and location of door openings in Presidio buildings. Each of the soldier's dwellings has an ordinary door in the front as well as in the rear wall. The door to the front of the church is arched; arched doorways also are indicated at the entrance to the corrals, to the bastion, and in one or two other places. The significance of the square door symbol on the plan, when it projects outward from the front wall of the *comandancia* is unknown (see figures 9 and 10).

The front door [plaza side] of El Cuartel measures 2' 9" x 6' 3". The lintel above the door is 7' long and 7 ½" thick, placed above the door opening to support the thick wall above the door.

Windows in El Cuartel are 2' wide and 3' high with a lintel 4' long and 5 ½" thick. Since the Goycoechea Plan shows no

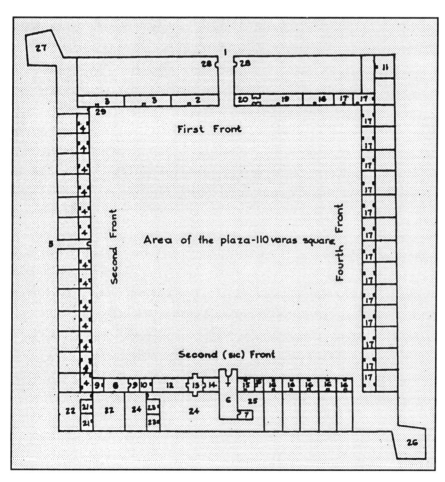

Figure 9: Goycoechea Plan for the Santa Barbara Presidio; taken
from a document in The Bancroft Library.

NOTES

Of the thirteen houses shown on the fourth front of the quadrangle, the walls are finished -- three-quarters [of a vara*] thick, and three varas high without the ridge of the roofs, which are to be the same as the other [houses] for the soldiers, and also the corresponding woodwork has been put into seven of them, and the little that is lacking for the rest is being brought, and more than four thousand tiles are made for their roofs.

All of the outer wall shown in this plan is ready to be built, and it will be started beginning with the month of November, at which time the quadrangle will be completed.

The front walls of the first front are standing; they are one and a half adobe [bricks] thick, mortared, because of the poor quality of the soil for adobes.

1. Main gate with an opening of 4 varas.

2. A storehouse for supplies, 20 varas in length and 5 1/2 in width, its roof of beams, finished boards, and good quality tile.

3. Two of the same, of the same size, for provisions and other effects, the roof of beams, wattles, and tile as above.

4. Thirteen houses for families -- 8 varas in length and 5 in width -- the roofs of rafters, wattles and good tile.

5. Private gate with an opening of 3 varas, roofed like the houses.

6. Church, 20 varas in length, 8 in width, and 7 1/2 in height, lined with mortar and white-washed -- its roof of beams and finished boards and good tile, and adorned with painting.

7. Sacristy, 5 varas in length and 4 in width.

8. Living-room of the second lieutenant, 8 varas in length, 5 in width -- its roof of rafters, wattles, and good tile.

9. Two bedrooms for the above -- 5 varas in the clear -- roof like the living-room.

10. Bedroom of the Comandante -- 5 varas in the clear, its roof of beams, finished boards and good tile.

11. House for the sentry.

12. A living-room for the Comandante, 11 varas in length and 5 in width, its roof of beams, finished boards and good tile.

13. Entrance hall of the above - 4 varas in the clear -- 4 in height, whitewashed on the inside, 3 1/2 varas in height.

14. Office for writing, 5 1/2 varas in length, 5 in width, whitewashed on the inside, 3 1/2 varas in height.

15. Living-room and bedroom of the chaplain, 11 varas in length for both rooms, and 5 in width -- the roofs of rafters, wattles and good tile.

16. Five houses for families -- 8 varas in length, 5 in width -- their roofs like that of the chaplain.

17. Fifteen houses on the fourth front for families -- 9 varas in length and 5 in width -- their roof like those before-mentioned.

18. House of the sergeant, 15 varas in length, 5 1/2 in width, its roof as above.

19. Barracks for the soldiers -- 20 varas in length, 5 1/2 in width, its roof as above.

20. Guard-house -- 12 varas and two small cells of 4 varas.

21. Kitchen and pantry of the second lieutenant, 6 varas in length and 4 in width, its roof as above.

22. Two yards for the second lieutenant's house -- one of 14 varas and the other of 7.

23. Kitchen and pantry of the Comandante -- 6 varas in length and 4 in width, roofed as above

24. Two yards for the Comandante -- one of 25 varas in length and 14 in width, and the other 14 in length and 8 in width.

25. Yard of the chaplain's house, 14 varas in length and 11 in width.

26. Bastion facing the west, of 6 varas.

27. The same, facing the east of 6 varas.

28. Gates to two corrals for stock -- 60 varas in length and 14 in width.

29. Gates or passage-ways to enter the bastions -- 2 1/2 varas in width.

Royal Presidio of Santa Barbara, September 16, 1788

Felipe de Goycoechea.

With grateful acknowledgement of the kind assistance of the Reverend Fr. Maynard Geiger, O. F. M.

(signed) *Mrs. Geraldine V. (Melville) Sahyun, Translator*

*[a vara = approximately 33"]

Figure 10: Translation by Geraldine V. (Melville) Sahyun of the notes to the Goycoechea Plan for the Santa Barbara Presidio; these notes are identical to those on the Fages Plan.

symbol for windows, the question has been raised as to whether there were any. Russell Ruiz pointed out that Mrs. Angustias de la Guerra Ord, daughter of a prominent *comandante* of the Presidio, in describing the Indian revolt of 1824, stated that Padre Ripoll, who had taken refuge at the Presidio, "was in a room which had a window toward the Mission."[31] Apparently Father Ripoll was staying at the *comandancia* since later Fr. Antonio Jayme came to the Presidio and Mrs. Ord stated, "the priests stayed on at our house."[32] Conceivably, of course, the *comandancia* might have had windows and other dwellings only doors; but logic favors a window in the front and rear wall of each residence.

Hawley says "the windows were merely small openings in the side of the walls which could be closed by wooden shutters."[33] As indicated in the chapter on Presidio Design, rear windows in the residences were an essential element in the defense of the Presidio, providing a protected defense post if Indians surmounted the defense wall.

Assuming windows did exist, they certainly had no window glass for a long time after the Presidio was completed.[34] Rawhide, scraped thin and made translucent by oil, kept the wind and the rain out and let the light in, and shutters were used for security and in foul weather.

In order to obtain the maximum amount of light from a given opening, window openings splayed out on the inside. The window sash, when present, was close to the outside of the wall. The sill was level, as was the top of the opening, but the sides of the opening were perhaps a foot wider on the inside (depending on the thickness of the wall) than on the outside. The sides of the opening were then whitewashed to

---

[31]Ord, *Occurrences in Hispanic California* p. 8.

[32]Ord, *Occurrences in Hispanic California*, p. 9.

[33]Hawley, *Early Days of Santa Barbara*, p. 36.

[34]Subsequent research has shown that window glass was available in Alta California during the late 18th century, but no direct evidence for its use at the Santa Barbara Presidio has been found to date. *Ed. note.*

reflect into the room the light from the outside. The same treatment was given some doors.

WALL PLASTER

An exterior plaster coat made from lime or cement apparently does not bond well with adobe bricks due, according to Long, to the difference in thermal expansion between the two materials or to their difference in ability to absorb moisture.[35] In any event, the sight of an adobe wall on which plaster has flaked off is so common that the phenomenon is sometimes faked to give the impression of age.

Because of this characteristic, two methods of improving the bond were incorporated in early structures. At Purísima Mission the method used in the building constructed after the 1812 earthquake is described by Hageman as follows:

> Since there is no bond between adobe brick (earth) and the lime plaster, mechanical means were resorted to in order to attach the plaster to the wall...First the adobe brick wall was scored with grooves about one and one-half inches wide and about the same in depth, generally diagonally, about eight inches on center. These grooves were then filled with lime mortar and chips of roof tiles, so that the surface was about flush with the adobe. This forms the bonding surface for the plaster coat which is then applied to about one-half inch in thickness over the adobe. Examination of the cross section of samples of plaster show that the finish surface (about one-eighth inch deep) is of a richer mixture of lime than the rest. This indicated that the plastering was done in two operations, first the three-to-one mortar mixture was applied, then followed up with a finishing coat, much as a modern "putty coat" is employed to secure a smoother finish.[36]

At the Santa Barbara Presidio, one reference to exterior plastering was found. Under date of February 3, 1787, *Comandante* Goycoechea reported to Governor Fages that

---

[35] Long, *Adobe Construction*, p. 43.

[36] Hageman and Ewing, *Mission La Purísima Concepción*, pp. 93-94.

"the people are riprapping the existing walls with mortar in order to prevent the rain from eroding the adobe."[37] The word "riprapping" is usually applied to the facing of a dam or the walls of a channel containing water, such as a canal or river embankment. The verb in Spanish is *ripiar*, which in the Velázquez dictionary means "to fill up the chinks of a wall with small stones or mortar."

The method involved placing small stones and broken chips of tile in the mud mortar between the adobe bricks while it is still wet. The "rubble" (another word for riprap) sticks out from the face of the adobe wall. When a lime mortar is plastered on the surface of the wall, it adheres to the small stones and pieces of tile, keeping the plaster from slipping down, even though the bond with the adobe is slight or nonexistent. When this technique is used in the joints between stones in a building or wall made of stone, it is called *rejoneado*.[38]

The Annual Report for Mission Santa Barbara dated December 31, 1794, in describing a granary and weaving room built during the preceding year, states:

> The whole is roofed with tile, and the crevices in the walls are for the most part filled in with small stones and mortar, and then plastered with mortar on the outside.[39]

An unsigned report dated August 6 and 9, 1791, to José Argüello, acting governor and *Comandante* of the Monterey Presidio, concerning instructions on building construction gave directions on the way a church, various walls, doors, corrals, patio, forge and rooms should be built. The report indicated the class of materials which should be employed and the nature of the *enjarramiento*.[40] *Enjarre* is a mix of mortar of mud and straw used to plaster the walls when they are

---

[37]Provincial State Papers, VII, 66.
[38]McAndrew, *The Open Air Churches of Sixteenth Century Mexico*, p. 190.
[39]Egenhoff, *Fabricas*, p. 155.
[40]Provincial State Papers, X, 43.

made of reeds or similar material. A detailed description of how the outside walls of an adobe structure were plastered, using cactus juice and oval-shaped stones to obtain a "polished" finish, is given by Hageman.[41]

The walls of a building are more visible to people than any other part of the structure. Since the workmen who constructed the Presidio—soldiers, sailors and neophyte Indians—were mostly unskilled, the walls were not perfectly plumb, nor the corners exactly 90 degrees. Therein lies the unique beauty and character of the adobe structures of that period, because a rough texture was created, only partially smoothed by application of the protective lime plaster coat. After the plaster had been applied and had dried, the walls were whitewashed, resulting in the neat, clean appearance commented upon by Vancouver in 1793.

Lack of construction skills caused serious problems of wall and roof failures, necessitating constant repair. On March 11, 1801, Governor Arrillaga informed the Viceroy that:

> the church of Port Monterey and other works are in ruins: the work of 20 years of the troops, Indians and townspeople, in repairs and construction is useless because of the haste and weakness with which they were made; and...it is necessary that construction in Monterey and San Diego begin again and with greater strength.[42]

On March 4, 1792, Acting *Comandante* Sal of the San Francisco Presidio wrote to Governor Roméu:

> In the rain which came in the month of January of 1779, two storehouses, the casemate, church, Commander's house, six houses of the troops, and the most and best of the four sides of the wall collapsed, so that at the end of the year 1780 there did not exist one house of those which had been erected up to the year 1778. The lack of intelligent workmen for the construction and direction of the works has contributed greatly to this situation, and at present

---

[41]Hageman and Ewing, *Mission La Purísima Concepción*, p. 94.
[42]Provincial State Papers, XXI, 59.

we are lacking them. The adobe is bad in and of itself, since with only the humidity it crumbles, and thus it is absolutely necessary that the roofs toward the south and southeast cover the greater part of the walls. [The destructive storms were from the south and southeast, as at Santa Barbara, necessitating the construction of overhanging eaves and roofed porches on those sides of the buildings]. It would be well to call the attention of the superiors to the fact that this Presidio has been built three times, with that which exists today, considering that in the year '80 and '81, the troops rebuilt a house of paling to shelter themselves with their families.[43]

Similar, but not as serious, damage occurred at the Santa Barbara Presidio, both from rain and from earthquake shocks. These catastrophes required either rebuilding or buttressing, or both. Buttress foundations were found at the northeast, northwest and southwest corners of the Presidio Chapel,[44] and what appears to be a buttress foundation was found at the middle of the west wall. This foundation is 4'x 4' and, if it supported a buttress, it was no longer needed by 1855 when James Alden painted a view of the west wall showing no buttresses.

The buttress at the northwest corner does show in the painting. Apparently it was triangular in shape and sloped upward from its outer edge to a point about 15 feet up the wall from the ground. It is believed that all buttresses were of stone, bonded together with lime mortar. Archaeological excavations have not progressed to the point where it can be stated that buttresses were used to support any walls other than those of the chapel.

Roof Construction

The description of the Presidio by Goycoechea states that the quarters of the *alférez*, the chaplain, sergeant's quarters,

---

[43]Provincial State Papers, XI, 233-37.
[44]Since this writing, evidence of a buttress at the southeast corner of the Chapel has also been discovered. *Ed. note.*

soldiers' barracks and 33 soldiers' family quarters had roofs of "*marrillos,* wattles and good tile." In contrast, the chapel, storehouses and *comandancia* had roofs of "beams, finished boards and good tile." The word *marrillo* translates as a short, somewhat heavy timber, indicating a structural system of smaller members, similar to modern 4" x 6" rafters in some buildings, and beams with ceiling planking in others. Kenneally translates what he read as *morillo* as "building frames" where it was used in a 1798 letter by Lasuén describing progress in construction at Mission San Luis Rey.[45]

It would seem logical to assume that in the building where a finished appearance was desired, namely the chapel and *comandancia,* and in the storehouses where the loft could be used for storage, beams spanned the room from wall to wall. On top of the beams, adzed or sawn planks were placed to form a ceiling of the room and, in the case of the warehouses, a floor for the loft. Elsewhere, where appearance was not critical, they had what we now call open-beam ceilings, in which a cross beam and a center post are used to support the ridgepole. In both cases roof-rafters were used to create the pitch of the roof. Wattles (willow withes or reeds) were attached to the rafters with rawhide, and the tiles were supported by the wattles. On top of the wattles there was probably placed a layer of mud, both as an added protection against leakage during storms and as a means of keeping the tile from slipping off the roof. Additionally, if the appearance of the roof in the *comandancia* in the Alden painting is correctly interpreted, there were longitudinal beams, or purlins, at the center point and at the plate line, in addition to the ridgepole, as shown in figure 11. These beams would have been supported by the cross walls and probably by posts on the cross beams.

In small structures a simple cross beam spanning the room

---

[45]Kenneally, *Writings of Lasuén,* II, 89-90.

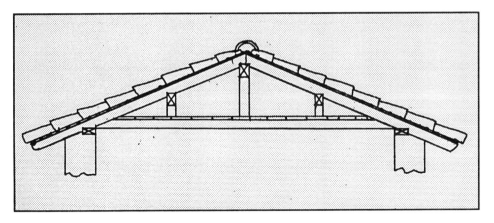

Figure 11

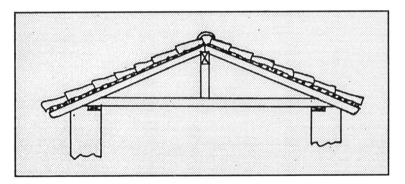

Figure 12

supported a vertical post which, in turn, supported the ridge beam, as shown in figure 12.[46]

The rafters and beams did not rest directly on top of the adobe walls at La Purísima Mission. A sill or plate 4½" x 10" was laid in the wall and plastered over.[47]

---

[46]Some changes in the language of this section were contributed by Norman Caldwell to clarify roof construction details. *Ed. note.*

[47]Hageman and Ewing, *Mission La Purísima Concepción*, p. 89.

There is no indication, such as a foundation in the middle of the room, that a center support post was used under the ceiling joist or to support the ridge beam, although, of course, all the possible locations for such a foundation have not been excavated. Such a support was used at the Pala Asistencia (a sub-mission of San Luis Rey). Newcomb wrote:

> Truthfully speaking, there are to be found in the missions no real trusses, in the modern sense. Attempts are found here and there, but a full accomplishment was never attained, due either to the ignorance of the *padres* regarding the principles of truss construction or the scarcity of iron for tensional members. The churches were usually spanned with heavy beams, which often carried also the roofing timbers above. In order to reinforce these beams, heavy corbels were introduced at their ends. Thus it will be seen that the width of the church was always conditioned by the length of the timbers obtainable, and, as a consequence, long narrow naves resulted.
>
> When "trusses" were introduced, they were usually poorly constructed, as was the case at Pala Chapel, where, the tensional members having been omitted, it was necessary to introduce a post at the center to prevent failure when the full weight of the heavy tile roof became effective. The tensional members have been supplied in recent years and the posts removed, greatly improving the interior of the church.[48]

In the Annual Report for San Diego Mission for 1779, Lasuén stated:

> We have transported the greater part of the lumber which was cut last year in the San Luis Rey Valley for the building of the church. We notice, however, that it is not the quality that can sustain the roof without the aid of supports at the center. On the other hand, our plan is to build it without any impediment or disfigurement of that kind.[49]

A photograph entitled "The original decoration on the

---

[48]Newcomb, *Old Mission Churches*, pp. 81-82.
[49]Kenneally, *Writings of Lasuén*, II, 342-43.

walls of the sanctuary of the chapel at Pala" shows a cross beam at the altar rail supporting a single post between the beam and the ridgepole.[50] The cross beam is supported by two posts, one on each side of the gateway in the altar rail.

In summary, it can be seen that methods of construction were pragmatic. Serious limitations existed, ranging from lack of skilled artisans, rudimentary plans, and scarcity of building materials of prime necessity. Nevertheless, despite rudimentary materials and methods of construction, Spanish colonial residents, with the help of local natives, built some important buildings that helped meet the essential requirement of holding the most northwesterly province of New Spain as a part of the overseas empire. The construction was appropriate to the area and in many ways dictated by such limited resources as the province provided. It justly deserves the characterization of being called California Franciscan architecture, though it might also be properly termed early California military construction.

---

[50]Webb, *Indian Life at the Old Missions*, opposite p. 223.

Epilogue

The story of the Santa Barbara Presidio is an interesting blend of science, history, and the arts. It provides an opportunity to bring together the skills of historical archaeology and documentary research in what is clearly a case study of the use of both of those specialties to tell a story which has been buried. The job has been to dig, both in the very center of the City of Santa Barbara and in the widespread archives. Both efforts have yielded highly useful material, the sort of information concerning the area's rich past that invites continued efforts. As a result of the newly uncovered material, *Citadel on the Channel* now tells a story which has been muted by dynamic growth of the city and by relative neglect of its past.

There is no doubt that this is not the last word to be said on the subject of the adobe presidio which long ago held a large area under its protection and guardianship. There should also result from this research the stimulus not only to add to the present study by continued excavation, but also to seek additional documentation, and other artifacts appropriate to interpretation of Santa Barbara's presidio. Other cities which had a Spanish presidio in their early history may well follow suit and profit from the example set by Santa Barbara.

Several factors have made the study of the "Citadel on the Channel" possible. As one of the last of the presidios founded in the Spanish Borderlands, it had the advantage of being started in a time when, for various reasons, more letters changed hands between the frontier and the viceroyalty, and letters from lesser persons are available. As a result, a surprisingly great amount of documentation has survived and the contents of these records brought to bear on the subject. This adds dimension not only to the historical record but also to the resources available for archaeology and subsequent reconstruction. Since construction of the Santa Barbara Presidio was late in the colonial period and it was the last of the California presidios to be planned and built, there is the advantage of researchers using the history of earlier presidial structures, and of the builders of yesteryear profiting from the experiences of their colleagues who had constructed with less guidance the three earlier Alta California presidios.

Another advantage is that the Santa Barbara Presidio was founded in an area of benign climate, which permitted the buildings to have occupancy long after their military importance disappeared. Also, the long tenure of its various commandants has been an asset insofar as biographical treatment of some of the persons, such as Felipe de Goycoechea, and later José de la Guerra, will lead to continued finds about operation of the presidio and the problems faced by the senior officer involved.

There still remain topics which have not yet been treated, or have been left with only a passing mention. Thus far little has been said about the social life centering around the presidio. Nor has there been treatment of the Presidio as a center of military command. The latter study will bring forth the day-by-day deployment of troops, as well as the many special assignments which were incumbent upon soldiers serving on the fringe of civilization—the last Spanish frontier, that of California. A fact which sets the California presidios apart from their counterparts elsewhere in the Borderlands is the possibility, realized from the beginning, that these bastions could some day be targets of attack from more sophisticated enemies than the Indians who were the probable attackers of presidios in Arizona, Sonora, New Mexico, Nueva Vizcaya, and Texas. In Alta California, the thickness of walls might be tested by cannon fire from oceangoing vessels or from large guns placed ashore for attack operations.

As fortresses, the California Presidios had a dual function, and this is exemplified by that of Santa Barbara. Defense, as reflected in the documents, was for two obvious purposes. Early documentation demonstrates the importance of occupying the Santa Barbara Channel to keep open communication and supply lines between the capital in Monterey with its northern dependencies, and the southern missions and their supporting presidio at San Diego. The narrowness of the coastal plain and the configuration of the nearby mountains dictated in large measure that the location finally chosen was almost foreordained for selection. Certainly there were more fertile areas, ones more capable of local support of a military mission. The local area lacked many of the obvious resources that would have made construction easier, most evident of which was scarcity of timber of sufficient size and utility to provide major structural pieces for the proposed buildings. Even the mission which later developed nearby was not ideally suited for it functions. Control of the Chumash Indians, the local residents who were culturally more advanced than most of their neighbors, was a factor in both Presidio and Mission establishment in an area of population concentration.

With establishment of the Presidio, it was possible to expand the missionary activity in the general area by creation of new missions which were supported by the Citadel on the Channel. Just as in the case of the mission, which a modern generation confuses with the sanctuary buildings which remain in refurbished, reconstructed or restored versions, there is an equal misconception of the presidio as being the four strong walls of a military bastion. It was more than that; it contained interior and exterior buildings. In the former category were the chapel, the commandant's quarters, the rooms and apartments of the other personnel attached to the garrison, and the logistic support storehouses for supplies and provisions.

Gun batteries had to have ammunition, which in turn required safe storage. Military residents needed to have small plots of land within the presidio walls for household activities and for efforts at self-sufficiency. Offices for military records, pay, and everyday activities were also needed. In the second category, somewhat limited because of potential exposure, were the extramural support facilities. First to mind was the construction of a gun battery for protection of the harbor and to repel any alien attackers from the sea. Commanding the anchorage, such as it was, when the gun battery was finally established, required the deployment of personnel, items for support of its function, and minor amenities that such semi-detached duty necessitated. Other extramural items were places for grazing and tending the rather substantial herd of horses that the regulations required each soldier to have available. To this was added oversight of a substantial number of mules, animals almost exclusively associated with the presidios and mainly used for pack trains hauling goods between establishments along the Camino Real, the colonial highway which later became U.S. Federal Highway 101. Oxen also formed a part of the military ranch to which a few soldiers were assigned.

Several other small outbuildings, corrals and special areas were set aside for military use, supporting the operation that was the principal mission of the Spanish soldiery. The military itself was composed mostly of men recruited on the frontier who demonstrated an aptitude for cavalry operations, for most of California's soldiers were buckskin-clad, informally trained dragoons. Later these troops were supplemented by a few enlisted men who had artillery training, whose collateral job was to impart their special knowledge to some of the basically cavalry troops at the presidios. All served a minimum of ten years, the regular initial enlistment.

Officers came from a variety of backgrounds, some being Spaniards, others being New World-born (*criollos*) and others coming from among the leading frontier families. To the officers and their commander (the Governor) and to the Franciscans at the missions (particularly the head of those grey-robed missionaries), we owe a great debt for providing us with the documentation which is used in our present studies. Their routine reports to superior authority form an important source of information which has been used in telling the story of the Santa Barbara Presidio. Another source is the special letters and reports of the same individuals in the form of the complaints of one or the other group. From these documents we obtain otherwise unavailable information about problems, friction, and self-congratulation. The special reports are less likely to be objective and must be used by the researcher with some caution.

This is not the complete story, nor is it presented as being typical of presidio planning, birth, growth and decline. Rather it is a stepping stone for complete understanding of one such presidio, the Citadel on the Channel at Santa Barbara. We hope it will be a springboard for continued efforts on the Presidio as an institution, and a stimulus for additional research activity which in turn will add to the present knowledge of the Santa Barbara Presidio in its many-faceted character.

DONALD C. CUTTER

Sources

Archival Collections

Archives of California. Transcripts in The Bancroft Library, Berkeley.
    Provincial Records, vols. I-IV.
    Provincial State Papers, vols. II-VII, IX-XII, XV-XVII, XX-
        XXI.
    Provincial State Papers, Benicia Military, vols. III-V, IX,
        XII, XIV, XVII, XX, XXI.
    State Papers, Missions, vols. I, II, VI.
    State Papers, Presidios I.
    State Papers, Sacramento, vols. I, IV.
Archivo General de la Nación, México, D.F.
    Provincias Internas, tomos 121, 122.
    Audiencia de Guadalajara, tomo 518.
    Obras Públicas, tomo 15.
    Archivo General de Simancas.
Newberry Library, Chicago.
    Richman Papers.
Santa Barbara Mission Archive-Library, Santa Barbara.
    California Mission Documents.
    Junípero Serra Collection.
    De la Guerra Papers.
    Santa Barbara Mission Registers.
    Santa Barbara Presidio Registers.

Books

Baer, Kurt. *Architecture of the California Missions.* Berkeley and Los Angeles, 1958.

Balls, Edward K. *Early Uses of California Plants.* Berkeley and Los Angeles, 1962.

Bancroft, Hubert H. *History of California,* 7 vols. San Francisco. 1886-90.

Beilharz, Edwin A. *Felipe de Neve: First Governor of California.* San Francisco, 1971.

Beittel, Will. *See*: Muller, Broder and Beittel.

Bolton, Herbert E. *Fray Juan Crespí, Missionary Explorer on the Pacific Coast.* Berkeley, 1927.

_____. *Font's Complete Diary: A Chronicle of the Founding of San Francisco.* Berkeley, 1931.

Bolton, Herbert E. (trans.). *Palóu's Historical Memoirs of New California*, 4 vols. Berkeley, 1926.

Brewer, William H. *Up and Down California in 1860-1864.* New Haven, 1930.

Brinckerhoff, Sidney B. and Odie B. Faulk. *Lancers for the King.* Phoenix, 1965.

Broder, Richard E. *See*: Muller, Broder and Beittel.

Brooks, Benjamin. *See*: Gidney, Brooks and Sheridan.

Brown, Allan K. *The Aboriginal Population of the Santa Barbara Channel.* Berkeley, 1967.

Caballería y Collel, Juan. *History of the City of Santa Barbara, California.* Santa Barbara, 1892.

Chapman, Charles E. *The Founding of Spanish California, 1687-1783.* New York, 1916.

_____. *A History of California: The Spanish Period.* New York, 1936.

Chatelain, Verne E. *The Defenses of Spanish Florida, 1565 to 1763.* Washington, 1941.

Cleland, Robert G. *Cattle on a Thousand Hills.* San Marino, 1941.

Cutter, Donald C. *Malaspina in California.* San Francisco, 1960.

Dana, Richard Henry. *Two Years Before the Mast*, 2 vols. Los Angeles, 1964.

Di Peso, Charles C. *The Sobaipuri Indians of the Upper San Pedro River Valley, Southeastern Arizona.* Dragoon, AZ, 1953.

Duflot de Mofras, M. *Exploration de Territoire de L'Orégon, des Californies et de la Mer Vermeille.* Paris, 1844.

Egenhoff, Elisabeth L. *Fabricas.* San Francisco, 1952.

Eldredge, Zoeth Skinner (ed.). *A History of California*, 5 vols. New York, 1914-1915.

Engelhardt, Fr. Zephyrin, O.F.M. *Missions and Missionaries of California*, 4 vols. San Francisco, 1908-1915.

_____. *San Buenaventura, the Mission by the Sea.* Santa Barbara, 1930.

_____. *Mission San Fernando Rey*. San Francisco, 1921.

Ewing, Russell C. *See*: Hageman and Ewing.

Faulk, Odie B. *See*: Brinckerhoff and Faulk.

Geiger, Fr. Maynard J., O.F.M. *The Life and Times of Junípero Serra*, 2 vols. Washington, 1959.

_____. *Mission Santa Barbara, 1782-1965*. Santa Barbara, 1965.

Geiger, Fr. Maynard J., O.F.M. (trans.). *Palóu's Life of Fray Junípero Serra*. Washington, 1955.

Gerald, Rex E. *Spanish Presidios of the Late Eighteenth Century in Northern New Spain*. Santa Fe, 1968.

Gidney, Charles M., Benjamin Brooks, and Edwin M. Sheridan. *History of Santa Barbara, San Luis Obispo and Ventura Counties, California*. Chicago, 1917.

Grant, Campbell. *The Rock Paintings of the Chumash*. Berkeley and Los Angeles, 1965.

Hageman, Fred C. and Russell C.Ewing, *An Archaeological and Restoration Study of Mission La Purísima Concepción* (edited by Richard S. Whitehead). Santa Barbara, 1980.

Harrington, John P. *Exploration of the Burton Mound at Santa Barbara, California*. Washington, 1928.

Hawley, Walter A. *The Early Days of Santa Barbara, California*. New York, 1910.

Hittell, Theodore H. *History of California*. 4 vols. San Francisco, 1885-1887.

Horne, Kibbey M. *A History of the Presidio of Monterey, 1770 to 1970*. Monterey, 1970.

Johnson, John E. (trans.). *Regulations for Governing the Province of the Californias*. San Francisco, 1929.

Kelsey, Harry. *Juan Rodríguez Cabrillo*. San Marino, 1986.

Kenneally, Fr. Finbar, O.F.M. (trans. and ed.). *Writings of Fermín Francisco de Lasuén*, 2 vols. Washington, 1965.

Long, J.D. *Adobe Construction*. Berkeley, 1946.

McAndrew, John. *The Open Air Churches of Sixteenth Century Mexico*. Cambridge, 1965.

Mason, Jesse D. (ed.). *History of Santa Barbara County, California*. Oakland, 1883.

Moorhead, Max. *The Presidio*. Norman, 1975.

Muller, Katherine K., Richard E.Broder, & Will Beittel *Trees of Santa Barbara*. Santa Barbara, 1974.

Newcomb, Rexford. *The Old Mission Churches and Historic Houses of California*. Philadelphia and London, 1925.

O'Neill, Owen H. (ed.). *History of Santa Barbara County*. Santa Barbara, 1939.

Ord, Angustias de la Guerra. *Occurrences in Hispanic California*. Washington, 1956.

Phillips, Michael J. *Santa Barbara County, California*. San Francisco, 1927.

Richman, Irving B. *California Under Spain and Mexico*. Boston and New York, 1911.

Sahyun, Geraldine V. (trans.), and Richard S.Whitehead, (ed.). *The Voyage of the Frigate Princesa to Southern California in 1782*. Santa Barbara, 1982.

Sheridan, Edwin. *See*: Gidney, Brooks and Sheridan.

Simmons, Marc. *Spanish Government in New Mexico*. Albuquerque, 1968.

Sloane, Eric. *A Museum of Early American Tools*. New York, 1964.

Storke, Yda Addis. *A Memorial and Biographical History of the Counties of Santa Barbara, San Luis Obispo and Ventura, California*. Chicago, 1891.

Sudworth, George B. *Forest Trees of the Pacific Slope*. Washington, 1908.

Thurman, Michael E. *The Naval Department of San Blas: New Spain's Bastion for Alta California and Nootka, 1767-1798*. Glendale, 1967.

Tibesar, Fr. Antonine, O.F.M. (ed.). *The Writings of Junípero Serra*, 4 vols. Washington, 1956-66.

Webb, Edith Buckland. *Indian Life at the Old Missions*. Los Angeles, 1952.

Whitehead, Richard S. (ed.). *See*: Sahyun and Whitehead.

_____. *See*: Hageman and Ewing.

Wilbur, Marguerite Eyer (trans.). *Duflot de Mofras' Travels on the Pacific Coast*, 2 vols. Santa Ana, 1937.

Wilbur, Marguerite Eyer (ed.). *Vancouver in California, 1792-1794, The Original Account of George Vancouver*, 2 vols. Los Angeles, 1954.

Periodicals and Reports

Bowman, J.N. "Weights and Measures of Provincial California." *California Historical Society Quarterly*, vol. 30, no. 4, 1951.

_____ "Adobe Houses of the San Francisco Bay Region." *The Geologic Guidebook of the San Francisco Bay Counties*. San Francisco, 1951.

Browne, Robert O. "San Buenaventura Mission Water System." Report submitted to Ventura City Council, 1974.

Carter, Charles Franklin (trans.). "Duhaut-Cilly's Account of California in the Years 1827-1828." *California Historical Society Quarterly*, vol. 8, no. 2, 1929.

Faulk, Odie B. "The Presidio: Fortress or Farce?" *Journal of the West*, vol. 8, no. 1, 1969.

Geiger, Fr. Maynard. "A Description of California's Principal Presidio, Monterey, in 1773." *Southern California Quarterly*, vol. XLIX, no. 3, 1967.

Parks, Marion (trans.). "Instructions for the Recruital of Soldiers and Settlers for California—Expedition of 1781." *Quarterly of the Historical Society of Southern California*, vol. XV, part II, 1931.

Servín, Manuel P. "Symbolic Acts of Sovereignty in Spanish California." *The Americas*, vol. XIII, 1956-57.

Servín, Manuel P. (trans.). "Costansó's 1794 Report on Strengthening New California's Presidios." *California Historical Society Quarterly*, vol. 49, no. 3, 1970.

Webb, Edith. "Pigments Used by the Mission Indians of California." *The Americas*, vol. II, no. 2, 1945.

Whitehead, Richard S. "Alta California's Four Fortresses." *Southern California Quarterly*, vol. LXV, no. 1, 1983.

Index

Interior Provinces, 46, 57, 112; 1781 Neve regulations, 48; instructions to Rivera, 61-64, 82-83; Yuma uprising, 77; mention, 87, 94, 97, 102, 128

Crops: *see* Agriculture

De la Guerra y Noriega, José Antonio: 35, 175-76, 204

Domínguez, Joseph Antonio: 133

Domínguez, Joseph María: 133

Doors: Carmel, 103; Santa Barbara, 190-91, 193-94

Echeveste, Juan José de: 47

El Presidio de Santa Barbara State Historic Park: 12-13; *also see* Santa Barbara Presidio, Santa Barbara Presidio Reconstruction

El Príncipe (ship): 30, 56n, 83

Escoltas: 36, 71, 94

Fages, Pedro: Portolá expedition, 33, 36; Mission San Luis Obispo, 37; feud with Serra, 37, 46-47; recalled, 47; Catalan Volunteers, 69-70; Yuma uprising, 77, 102; Santa Barbara Presidio plan, 101, 114-16, 126, 129, 136; appointed governor, 102; Santa Barbara Mission, 102; Santa Barbara Presidio construction, 105, 125-141, 166, 183, 189, 194; Monterey Presidio, 182

Favorita (ship): 96, 105, 126, 129, 131

Feliz, Juana Vitala: 133

Feliz, Vitoreno: 133

Figuer, Juan: 58

Floor tiles: *see ladrillos*

Flores, Manuel: 135

Font, Pedro: 40

Foundations: construction, 181-85; Santa Barbara, 182, 186; Monterey, 182-83

Furnishings: Carmel, 103; Santa Barbara, 143

Gálvez, José de: colonization plan, 29-30; 1772 Regulations, 43-46; mention, 87, 105

Gálvez, Matías de: 127

Gigedo, Revilla: 141-42

Giménez, Hilario: 133

Glass: 175-76, 193

Gonzales, Diego: 99

Goycoechea, Felipe Antonio de: Santa Barbara Presidio plan, 19, 101, 114, 126, 129, 136, 156, 179-80, 189-92, 197-98; Santa Barbara Presidio *comandante*, 100, 102, 108, 125-49, 155, 166, 172, 183, 194, 204; military service, 100; Santa Barbara Mission founding, 102

Gratuity Fund: 145

Habilitado: see Paymaster

Hardware: 175, 179

Hijosa, Francisco: 135

Horses: mention, 61, 134; pasturage, 50, 110, 130, 206, brands, 99

Indian hostilities: San Diego, 31; Yuma uprising, 33, 65, 102; San Gabriel, 36; Rincón, 37; Dos Pueblos, 38; in Internal Provinces, 43, 110; 1824 revolt, 193

Indian labor: San Buenaventura, 80; Santa Barbara Presidio, 105, 129, 131, 136, 140, 144, 154-56, 159, 196; 1772 Regulations, 111; Santa Barbara Mission, 155-56; unskilled, 178

Internal Provinces: Indian hostilities, 43, 109-10; mention, 91, 128; area defined, 109; defenses, 109-11; jurisdiction change, 112; presidio ruins, 112-14

Jayme, Antonio: 193

Juana Maria: 134

Labor, construction: soldiers, 71, 80, 104, 110, 145, 196; servants, 71, 76; Indians, 80, 105, 111, 129, 131, 136, 140, 144, 154-56, 159, 178, 196; sailors, 126-27, 130, 132, 196; convicts, 127; *also see* Artisans

Ladrillos: mention, 87; Santa Barbara, 106n, 139, 152, 172-73; fabrication, 171-72; La Purísima Mission, 172; dimensions, 172

Lafora, Nicolás de: 43, 111